THE HAPPY MINIMALIST

HOW TO CREATE A SIMPLER, MORE ORGANIZED,
MORE MEANINGFUL MORE JOYFUL LIFE AND
ACHIEVE INNER PEACE BY GETTING RID OF
UNNECESSARY STUFF

MARC REKLAU

MAKLAU PUBLISHING

Disclaimer

This book is designed to provide information and motivation to our readers. It is sold with the understanding that the publisher is not engaged to render any type of psychological, legal, or any other kind of professional advice. The instructions and advice in this book are not intended as a substitute for counseling. The content of each chapter is the sole expression and opinion of its author. No warranties or guarantees are expressed or implied by the author's and publisher's choice to include any of the content in this volume. Neither the publisher nor the individual author shall be liable for any physical, psychological, emotional, financial, or commercial damages, including, but not limited to, special, incidental, consequential or other damages. Our views and rights are the same:

You must test everything for yourself according to your own situation talents and aspirations

You are responsible for your own decisions, choices, actions, and results.

Marc Reklau

❁ Created with Vellum

CONTENTS

"The secret of happiness, you see, is not found in seeking more, but in developing the capacity to enjoy less"

Socrates

INTRODUCTION

In this book, we'll not only talk about minimalism but also about the uncluttering—both physical and mental—that comes with it. I don't know what comes first. Do you decide to unclutter and then become a minimalist or do you decide to become a minimalist and therefore start to unclutter? As I said: I don't know. I guess it works both ways. I think for me, it started with uncluttering and then over time it turned into a minimalist lifestyle. There are fantastic side effects that come with it like gaining happiness, clarity, and time.

The minimalist was always strong within me even if I didn't notice it for many, many years.
I always had the feeling that I was happier with less stuff. My apartment in Germany where I lived for seven-plus years back in the nineties, according to my friend Martin, always looked like I just moved in or like I was just about to move out.

A bed, two chairs, a small table, a desk and office chair, a cupboard, a TV set, a DVD player, a stereo, and a PlayStation. That was it. It was awesome!

Nine years ago, I was jobless. Today I live my dream life in the beautiful city of Budapest—one of the most vibrant capitals of Europe. I'm doing what I love most: writing books, taking naps, going for long walks, traveling, watching Netflix (sometimes), and still having enough time to work 7 to 8 hour days. Actually, at the moment it's closer to four or five hour days.

How did I get there? Good habits, uncluttering and minimalism, patience, and hard work.
If you want a get quick rich scheme or need fast money, this book is not for you. Good things take time—and so does success.

It won't be easy, but it gets easier along the way.

Minimalism means to eliminate the unnecessary and focus on the essential. If you commit to this way of life, you'll find happiness, fulfillment, and freedom along the way.

Achieving minimalism is done like change is always done. In baby steps. These baby steps over time will amount to enormous change. The magic words are: Daily. Incremental. Changes.

At the beginning of all change is the decision to make change, and that decision has to be followed up with action right away. It has to be followed up with one step in the right direction. And then another one. And another one.

If you expect great new revelations on the subject of minimalism and uncluttering, I have to disappoint you. You won't find them in this book. What you will find is a mixture of different suggestions from many other minimalism and uncluttering books that I applied in my own life and that made my life a whole lot better, easier, and happier.

This is not a book about happiness despite its title. It's a book about minimalism and uncluttering. Nevertheless, I strongly believe that if you apply the exercises and concepts of this book in your life (the more, the better), then you will become happier in the process of doing it.

This will be a short book. Although reading this introduction, you might think the opposite. I won't describe to you how to clean your house over the span of 50 pages. What I will do is convince you to just do it. If you need more information on uncluttering like shopping lists, a description of room by room, drawer by drawer cleaning, then I recommend *10-Minute Declutter* by Steve (S.J.) Scott and Barrie Davenport. They describe in detail how you can move forward.

In 2003, I moved to Barcelona with one duffle bag. The second time I moved, I already needed three duffle bags. However, one taxi ride was enough to move my stuff. Then I met my (now ex-) wife, and when we moved again in 2011, we needed a small van and three trips to move our stuff.

My next move in 2018, I did alone again. I was moving to a boat, so I got rid of over half of my stuff using Mari Kondo's KonMari Method above all. However, I also used tricks I picked up from Steve (S.J.) Scott's and Barrie Davenport's book *10-Minute Declutter*, the minimalists, Joshua Becker's *Simplify*, and various blog posts. I moved to the boat mainly because I always wanted to live on a boat, but also to force myself to get rid of a lot of my stuff. I was already fully embracing the idea of "less is more."

In 2020, I moved again. This time I moved to the island of Malta by plane. At this point, I had to throw out even more stuff. And surprise, surprise, I was back down to a big and a small suitcase. So actually, one of the best ways to unclutter and get rid of stuff is moving. I had to smile in the Frankfurt airport, waiting for my flight to the beautiful island I would be making my new home. I was standing there with all of my belongings in one big and one small suitcase while people that were going on a two- or three-week vacation had more luggage than I had.

Unfortunately, my stay on the beautiful island of Malta was shorter than expected, so I moved again. I took one suitcase with me, and the other one was sent to me (sendmybag.com shipped it to my place in the center of Budapest within 24 hours). That was it. All my belongings fit in one and a half suitcases. I'll probably get it down to one by the time I move again in the future.

Anyways, enough about my moving history. The most important thing above all was not only reading the mentioned books but applying their teachings. The same will happen for you. If you only read this book, it will entertain you—well, at least that's what I hope. If you apply some of the things shared here, they may take your life to the next level.

Maybe you'll become happier than ever before, or you will feel a freedom you never felt before. I don't know. It's up to you.

Minimalism doesn't mean you have to live with nothing, that you have a certain number of items, or that all your belongings have to fit into one suitcase. It means you live simpler and with more purpose. I lived as a minimalist in a furnished 120 square meters (1300 sq. feet) penthouse. This didn't mean I'd turned my back on minimalism. It means I was still very mindful of what I bought. I kept my flat clutter-free. Though, I did make one mistake. I rented the flat thinking I'd get lots of visitors and need lots of space. Well—due to the Pandemic—most of the time, I was alone. In Budapest, I downsized again. Now, I have a 65 sqm flat, which is still more than enough space for one person and enough for two. The most important thing is to keep it free of clutter because clutter—physical and mental—distracts me from what really matters.

Before I come under suspicion of being one of Klaus Schwab's agents (that's the bonehead who says that by 2030, "you'll own nothing and will be happy"), let me be clear about something. I own close to nothing, and I'm very happy about it—but that's because it was MY CHOICE, not because some psychopathic millionaire and his corrupt henchmen have forced it on me. And that's a HUGE difference.

This is a short book. I figured it would be excessive to write a 200-page book on minimalism. Less is more.

I'm not going to pretend I invented a new system nor give it a fancy name. I just applied what Marie Kondo and other authors that have great books about cleaning systems teach. You should read them, too. Although if you APPLY what you learn in this book, you might not have to.

I noticed for me that the uncluttering goes better when I go room by room. Right now, I have the advantage that I arrived here with close to nothing and moved into a furnished apartment, so the challenge for me is slightly different: I already did the uncluttering. So, not my mantra is "don't accumulate too much stuff."

But this is not only about getting rid of unnecessary stuff—although it might start with it. With time you'll get better at decision-making and probably get rid of unnecessary emotions, unnecessary limiting beliefs, bad relationships, and bad business partners. That's the real miracle.
You'll gain mental clarity, and life will just get so much easier. You'll probably never want to go back to your old ways. And time . . . oh my . . . as you clear out the distractions, you'll gain so much more time.

Enough said!
Let's start the fun ride.

1

WHAT IS MINIMALISM?

Minimalism is about choices. About better choices. It's about having only the essentials and letting go of all the unnecessary things. It's also about choosing to say "No" to a lot of things so that we can enjoy the things we say yes to a lot more.

It's about embracing the "Less is more" and "quality over quantity." But above all, it's about the degree of minimalism that you are comfortable and happy with. There are no rules. Minimalism to me might be something totally different to me than it is to you. There is no one-size-fits-all approach. While there are minimalists who only have 100, 50, or even fewer items, my goal as a minimalist was to get rid of all the things I didn't really need. This process led to the result that I could now fit all my belongings into one big suitcase. Anyways, you can also be a minimalist living in a 2000 square feet flat, having only the necessary and gotten rid of the unnecessary.

Minimalism is not about getting things done. It's about getting the right things done. The important things. The things that drive you forward. The things that bring you closer to your goals. It's not about accumulating stuff. Spoiler alert: Having more will not make you happy, although billions in advertising dollars are spent to make you think exactly that. Minimalism is about getting rid of things and concentrating on the really important stuff. A great side effect of minimalism is that, together with the clutter, you might also get rid of the drama.

At best, minimalism will bring more joy, new meaning, more sense, new and better emotions, more time, more money, and better relationships to your life. At worst, nothing will change. So why not give it a shot. I'll show you how I became a minimalist and how it brought clarity, focus, and happiness into my life based on my experiences. Then you will be prepared to use it at your own will.

My goal is to provide you with habits and tools that bring you the same clarity and happiness while you eliminate all the unnecessary in your life. All kinds of clutter—the physical and the mental—that distracts you from what is really important shall go.

Once you adopt the minimalist mindset, nothing will ever be the same.

Let's go!!

2

CULTIVATING A MINIMALIST MINDSET

Becoming a minimalist undoubtedly also goes with watching less TV. It's a lot more difficult to unclutter and get rid of stuff when thousands of advertisements a day tell you to buy more.

Well, nowadays, advertisements are everywhere, even on our smartphones. So, by wanting less, you're going directly against the grain of a culture that tells us every day that we need to want more.

I don't fall for it anymore, but I'm not sure if that's because I became a minimalist or because I became a self-confident person with good self-esteem. I no longer have the emotional emptiness that I had to fill with constant buying anymore. I can wear a no-name T-shirt and feel fine. (Although I have to admit that I have lots of Nike T-shirts. I just love their slogan.)

Anyways. I think your minimalist mindset will build on the process. As you repeat the question, "Is this necessary?" "Does it spark Joy?" (Yes, I'm actually using this, and it works. Thanks, Marie Kondo!) so many times, sooner or later, you won't be able to get it out of your head anymore, and you'll start asking yourself the same questions while in the mall or on Amazon. And most of the time, the answer will be "NO." Voila.

You'll know you are on the right path when you stop organizing items and just give away those you don't need. Organizing is not minimizing. It's just putting things in a bin or a basket or tugging them away instead of making the decision, "Do I really need this?"
Usually, the best process here is to throw everything on the (clean) floor and go through the mountain item by item, asking the questions mentioned above, plus: "How many of these do I/we really need?"

Right now, I have four towels. Well, actually, I have two. Two came with the furnished flat I rent. I also have a washing machine and a dryer. So, in two hours, I have fresh towels again. And what about visitors, you ask? Well, that's the thing. I could have eight towels. The truth is, I don't get a lot of visitors so I'm good with four.

I also have only three sets of sheets per bed (two would be enough). They also came with the flat. But even if they were mine, I'd leave them behind when moving and just buy two new sets wherever I move.

This is what happens when you ask the question, "How much of this do we actually need?" You can fight against it; you can say it's false, but that doesn't change the fact: You can live with a lot less than you think.

This doesn't mean you can have nothing in your house or flat. I have three beautiful paintings in my living room. And yes, you guessed it. They came with the flat. Still, this does not mean you cannot have anything. You can have things. But they must be things you love and things that "spark joy." So minimalism doesn't mean getting rid of everything. It means getting rid of the unnecessary. This will create a lot of space for things that spark joy, that are useful, and that are beautiful. Useful in this case means, "Do you actually use them?" Not "do you think you will use them one day in the future?"

To make a long story short, to become a minimalist, you have to think like a minimalist. And most of the time, a minimalist will think, "Do I really need this?" "Is this useful?" "Do I love this?" Minimalists are focused on what they need and what they love.

3

BECOMING A MINIMALIST

Yes! I can feel the force of the minimalist is already strong within you because you're reading this book. So how do you become a minimalist? The short version is you read a lot of books on minimalism and then put the information into practice. That's it. Easy, eh?

Well, at least, that's what I did. Learning different things from each book, I found my own style—in the beginning, I was mostly influenced by Mari Kondo's book *The Magic of Tidying up*.

It also didn't happen overnight. It happened gradually. It all started with putting my cupboard in order, then the living room, the kitchen, the bathroom, and the office. So, I finally had my place in order, but I still had far too much stuff. Observing my cupboard, I noticed that I always put on the same six or seven T-shirts, and so the hidden minimalist inside me started asking some nagging questions, such as "Why do you need 30 T-shirts if you always wear the same ones?"

Soon, I began a new approach where I started to throw away things. That's where minimalism started for me—getting rid of stuff that I didn't need. I'll talk more about how I did that later.

Anyways reading lots of books about minimalism is not enough. You have to find your personal Minimalist style, and then the fun starts. What has to go? What do you decide to keep? This is very personal. While some can do without a toaster or a Nespresso coffee machine (yours truly included), others can't.

For example: For the longest time before starting my Minimalist journey, I had ten bath towels despite living alone. I actually always used the same two (because they were fluffier than the rest). One purge later, I had six.
Another purge later four. If I had gone hardcore, I would have kept only my favorite two (for my lovely girlfriend Natalia and me) because we rarely have people staying over. And if we move again, we'll leave the towels although it will be difficult to find towels that are as fluffy . . .

More important than the question "How do you become a minimalist?" is the question "WHY do you want to become a minimalist?" Because once you find your WHY, you will also find the HOW.

So WHY do you want to become a minimalist? Think about it and write it down here:

4

HOW TO CREATE A MINIMALISTIC HOME

This was meant to be a long chapter where I explain in detail
how to create your minimalist home and what that should look
like. I just read a chapter in another book on what a minimalistic
home should look like, and it totally put me off—and I consider
myself a minimalist, so I don't know what a chapter like this
would do to you.

At the same time, I thought to myself, "Who the heck am I to tell
you what YOUR minimalistic home should look like?" I'm not an
interior designer or decorator. I have absolutely no idea about
that. I have no idea about colors or how much furniture should
be in your minimalistic home.

I know what a minimalistic home looks like to me—when I lived
on a boat, the decisions practically took themselves. I also know a
cluttered home when I see one. Too much stuff in too little space.
Lack of space and lack of air to breathe.
So, I'll leave this up to you. I trust you'll know when your home is
minimalistic enough for you. Your minimalistic home will be at
the end of your decluttering process.

Ok, there are some things that a minimalistic home doesn't have, like stuff piled on surfaces and big stacks of newspapers—but you already threw those out in your uncluttering process, right? The mantra "Quality over quantity" also applies to your home. Add getting rid of duplicates and having clean surfaces to this, and your home is already looking quite minimalistic.

The most important question is, "**What does a minimalist home look like to you?**" And if it's a big colorful apartment that doesn't have clutter and feels minimalistic to you, then it might just be that.

5

THE DECISION TO BECOME A MINIMALIST

It's funny. We read so many books on how to change our lives, how to become happier, and how to have more time. We take the online course, go to the conference, talk to a coach. Sometimes nothing happens, and we go on in our old ways. And sometimes, the only thing it takes to change everything is to MAKE THE DECISION to change. Yup. It's that easy and yet that difficult. I've seen it so many times.

One of my clients had three goals: Buying an apartment, finding a serious girlfriend, and changing jobs. He hadn't achieved these goals in two years, although he's pretty handsome and had the money to buy an apartment. Five weeks after we started the coaching process, he had accomplished his first two goals. He bought an apartment and met a beautiful woman who now is his lovely wife and the mother of his two kids. I wish I could say that this was all due to my awesome coaching, but it wasn't. I'm convinced it happened because when signing me on as his coach and speaking out loud about his goals, making a plan, and working towards it—above all, it was his DECISION that got things rolling. For the first time, he was stating aloud: "I want to buy an apartment. I'm ready to meet the love of my life." That put things in motion. With his decision backed up by a strategy and an action plan, success was just a question of time.

Same thing with another client. Only the decision to work on himself and become even more successful—showing his commitment by working with a coach—made him more successful. In the last month of our work together, he had the best month ever in his business. Again, I'm convinced that the DECISION to become more successful and become the best version of himself did 80% of the work towards his success. It might sound like woo woo. But there are some things in life that can't be explained. Sometimes we have to show the universe / god / all that is that we are ready to receive.

This is something I've seen happening over and over again. I can't promise that it works 100% of the time, but I'll guarantee that it will not work if you don't even try.

So, make the decision to become a minimalist NOW.

6

LESS IS MORE

Yeah, I know. I bet you've heard that one before. It's also true.

Less stuff means more time, more money, more freedom, less stress, and less worries.
Once you embrace the "Less is more," you'll be well on the way to becoming a minimalist.

Minimalism has many advantages. For me, it's above all the mental clarity it gives me. Happiness and life just get so much simpler with fewer things.

I'm not great at cleaning, and still my house is always clean. Less stuff to dust, less rooms to clean. And believe me, it's super easy to clean an uncluttered floor and wipe off empty countertops.

For many people cleaning is moving stuff from one place to another and back.

Another biggie is shopping with purpose. Here's my trick. I love to buy at outlet malls. For a former shopping addict, that's dangerous grounds. Well, not anymore.

Usually, I already know what I need when I get there, and I'm also not an emotional shopper. I have no emotional holes to fill. I also don't buy anything in the first round. Yup, you heard right. So, I go through the whole mall once only, looking, taking mental notes of what I like. I might even make a list on my mobile phone.

Then I go on a second round. Funnily, 90% of the stuff I liked in the first round I either don't like anymore or don't need. So many times, I leave the mall without buying anything. This is great for my wallet and keeps my cupboards on a minimalist level.

A nice side effect is that as I don't spend money on things I don't need, I have a lot more money to spend on what I love, like traveling and experiences. I'm also debt-free—which adds to very good nights of sleep and having virtually zero stress most of the time.

So, minimalism is saying NO to mindless shopping and YES to mindful shopping. You only buy what you really need, and many times that's not a lot. I also don't fall for "sales." I only buy what I need. I don't buy things I don't need just because they are on sale. Keep this in mind. This could also happen gradually, but the more mindful you are about your shopping, the better you get at only buying what you need. A great side-effect is you'll have more money to pay off your debts.

Having less also means knowing what you have. When you have lots of stuff, this is not always the case. You probably forget a lot of the items you own. Knowing what you have means being able to find things. It's also knowing what you don't have. Remember the six boxes I left unopened for three years. Yeah. That won't happen anymore. If you know what you don't have, you don't waste time looking for it. You can just borrow, rent, or buy it. This will save you time and lots of stress.

Less stuff means more time. Less cleaning, less searching, and less putting things in order means more time for the things you love to do. I told you. It's magic. I can't wait until you start living the minimalist lifestyle. Not too long from now (hopefully), you will be telling me: "Marc! You were right. I've got so much more time now and feel a freedom I've never felt before."

Say "YES" to less is more and say bye-bye to being overwhelmed by your stuff.

BECOME DETACHED FROM MATERIAL BELONGINGS

Once you become detached from material belongings, life becomes a lot better. It's not easy because many times, there are underlying causes for our consumerism, like low self-esteem or some emotional emptiness that we may be trying to fill with shopping for useless things.

In my case, I don't know what came first. Did the inner healing and knowing that brands would not fill the vacuum and actually mean nothing lead me to minimalism, or was it the opposite. Did I learn and heal through my adoption of minimalism and the process of uncluttering? Who cares? Does it even matter? The end result is the same. I'm happy, feel a lot lighter, and going to the mall with me is no fun anymore because I hardly buy anything.

I don't need a big car to feel complete (but sometimes I rent one). I found out that for my lifestyle owning a house is not great. I would rather rent. (Two of my core values are Freedom and Independence, which should explain it.)

In my happiness studies, I found that it makes you a lot happier to spend money on experiences and people (this is NOT an invitation to ask me for money, so please don't. I choose the charities I give to) than on things.

Especially in the exciting times that we're living in, where things change so quickly, I prefer not to have a house or a mortgage to bog me down. Any political or societal changes I don't like. I pack my one suitcase and get a one-way ticket to a country that's more stable and/or treats me better. It's not pleasant, but it is what it is.

I found out that too much stuff only weighs me down, but as I said in the beginning: Minimalism is something totally different for everyone. In the end, I want this book to help you make your life better—if you want to, that is. If not, I hope that I at least entertained you.

THE BENEFITS OF MINIMALISM

Let's talk about the benefits of minimalism. Are you over-whelmed by the sheer volume of your material possessions? Does it take you a long time to find things? Do you know you have too much stuff but have no idea how to get rid of it or what to get rid of first? Have you heard about minimalists and how happy they are with less stuff? Do you know it's time to let go of some of your stuff, but you have no idea how? Or maybe you feel drained by your clutter. If you identify with any of the above or simply want to live a more organized lifestyle and have more time, this book is for you.

Need more motivation? Here are some of the countless benefits of living a minimalist lifestyle:

- You'll have more time. Fewer things equals less time for maintaining and organizing them and more time for the things you enjoy. You'll also become more productive.
- You'll have more money. You'll definitely spend less because you'll learn about your spending patterns, stop emotional purchases, and buy only the things you really need.

- You'll have more quality in your life. As "quality over quantity" becomes your mantra, you'll have leveled up your life because you own good stuff, not mediocre stuff.
- You feel FREE. As I mentioned before, I used to be weighed down by all my stuff. Now I feel free.
- You'll have less stress. Many times, without noticing—this happens subconsciously—a cluttered environment stresses us. The less clutter, the less visual stress. Many times, our environment reflects our inner state. If we feel depressed or stressed, it has a direct influence on how we keep our surroundings and the other way round. In a clean, organized environment creativity skyrockets.
- Your confidence will improve. When you look at your clean and clutter-free area, you'll feel a sense of accomplishment and even pride. You did it, and it feels great.
- You'll become more grateful for the things you have. After the process of decluttering, you'll only keep the things you love and appreciate most. The ones that "spark joy." You'll also learn to be more grateful for everything you already have in the process.
- You'll get rid of all the excess stuff and will only have what you really need. Energy will increase and flow freely.
- You might discover the real meaning of your life (spoiler alert: it's not accumulating stuff).
- You'll be an example. Once you tap out of consumerism and spend less, you are actually saving the planet. **You're actually DOING something.** Nowadays, everybody talks about how they want to improve the world and save the planet, but few people actually DO something. People glue their hands to the streets to "save the Planet," but then let Mummy pick

them up with her SUV and go home to their cluttered homes with 80% of their things they don't need.

- You'll improve your focus and clarity. Too much stuff distracts you. Yes, even visual distractions can distract you. With fewer distractions, you'll be better able to focus on the tasks at hand.
- You'll give back. Once you live the minimalist lifestyle, you'll have more money. You'll probably save so much money that you can give some of it away to good causes.
- You'll get a fresh start now and then. Sometimes when you're stuck and bogged down, the only thing it needs is a good purge and uncluttering to bring things back into motion. Whenever you want something new in your life, a change, start purging. The universe wants to fill empty spaces

Are you motivated yet? Then let's go!

9

MAKE MINIMALISM A GOAL AND FOLLOW THROUGH

Brian Tracy says that "People with clear, written goals accomplish far more in a shorter period of time than people without them can ever imagine." He is right! Once you set a goal, you'll know the direction you're going, and that's already 80% of the way to achieve it. The rest is patience and perseverance.

I avoided setting goals for the longest time in my life (many times, I set the wrong goals and achieved them). Since I began setting goals, my life has improved beyond my imagination. In the last seven years, I achieved my biggest dreams and a lot more than in the forty years before. It was not a walk in the park, but it was totally worth it. I didn't even reach all of my goals. Maybe not even half of them. And it's still better than any other time in my life. It's no surprise that the approximately 2 or 3% of people who set goals usually succeed.

So why doesn't everybody set goals? I guess many people just don't know about the power of goal setting; others are afraid of failure (or even success). The scary thing about having goals is that suddenly you can measure yourself against something. No need to be scared, though; if you go one step at a time and remain flexible, then over time, you can achieve things that you couldn't even imagine before. The best thing is it's not even about the goal. It's about the person you become on the way to your goal.

Goals will drive you to take action. They are like a GPS system leading the way. Goal setting becomes even more powerful if you write your goals down. It will help you concentrate and focus on the activities that bring you closer to your goal.

Ten-year goals, five-year goals, yearly goals, quarterly goals, monthly goals, daily goals, business goals, money goals, physical form goals, personal growth goals, romance goals, family goals, health goals, and travel goals. Is your head spinning already? Sorry for that. Don't worry; you don't have to do it all at once. You can start small.

Once you see how goal setting changes your life, you'll love it. With time and experience, you will come to the point where the question is not IF you reach your goal but WHEN.

Put your goals in writing. That's even more powerful. Looking at your written goals daily will drive you to take action and help you prioritize your actions.

So once you make "Living a Minimalist Lifestyle" your goal, you must dig deeper and find out what minimalism means to you and how that life will look. Is it having a minimum of everything? Is it decluttering your house?

Once you are clear about your goal and what it will look like, come up with the actions that help you on the way. I break down my goal-setting process in the next chapter.

For some people, it's helpful to share their goals with a friend to keep them accountable; for others, it isn't. You choose.

Oh. Yes. One more thing: **When pursuing your goal, reward yourself for the effort put in, and not just for the results.** Self-punishment is not allowed! Keep in mind that you are much further than you were a week or a month ago.

Ready? Let's do a little more goal setting in the next chapter.

GOAL SETTING CONTINUED . . .

In the last chapter, we talked a lot about goals and how they influence your life. I don't like long chapters so instead of one long chapter, here comes another short and quick one. This is how goal setting will look in practice. Just follow the steps.

1. Write down your goals. It shows commitment to your goals and will drive you to take action. It will help you focus on the activities that bring you closer to your goal. You'll also start making better decisions while focusing on where you want to go.
2. Be clear about your goals like "I'm going to increase sales by 5% by December 2023," "I'm going to run 5 miles four times a week by November 30, 2023."
3. Break them down into small achievable action steps and make a list of all the steps that you will take to get there. Calculate how long it will take you, and don't forget to set a deadline for each action step and goal.
4. Don't worry if you don't reach the goal by the exact date you've set; it's just a way of focusing on the goal and creating a sense of urgency. As I mentioned before, in the last few years, I have only reached half of the goals I've set or less. Still, these have been the best years

of my life, and now I'm working on the goals I didn't achieve last year.

5. Remember, the goals have to be yours, specific, stated positively, and you have to commit to them.

6. When pursuing your goals, you reward yourself for the effort put in, and not just for the results. Self-punishment is strictly forbidden!

7. Goals will not make you happier nor save you from failures, hardships, insecurities, or disappointments on the way to success—those are normal and inevitable. BUT: Meaningful goals will help you overcome these obstacles and keep you going and persisting on your way to success and happiness.

8. In my case, having a to-do list is extremely beneficial (some people might disagree). Put your action steps on it, as well as the time it takes to do the task, and put deadlines for each task.

9. Balance your goals (physical, economic, social, professional, family, and spiritual). Sometimes people thrive in one part of their lives at the cost of neglecting other parts. Find the balance.

Last but not least, I'll leave you the goal-setting exercise that is the foundation of everything I have today:
I want you to write down what you **want your life to look like** in 10 years (in 5 years, in 1 year, etc.) When you write it down, I want you to write down what you WANT, not what you think is possible. So GO BIG! There are no limits to your imagination.

1. What do you want your life to look like in 10 years? There are no limits! Go big!

2. What do you have to achieve in 5 years to get closer to your goal in 10 years?

3. What do you have to achieve in 1 year to get closer to your goal in 5 years?

4. What do you have to achieve in 3 months to get closer to your 1-year goal?
5. What are the things that you can do NOW to reach your 3-month goal?
6. Write down at least three things and TAKE ACTION!

11

MINIMALISM = MO' MONEY

Let's talk about a pretty awesome side effect of being a minimalist. If you buy less stuff, you'll end up having more money. Most people think that you become richer by earning more money. Usually, what happens is (and I'm guilty as charged) that the more money you earn, the more money you spend. The real secret to getting richer is spending less.

At one moment, you'll just don't care anymore to "keep up with the Joneses" or as in a variation of the famous quote sometimes attributed to Will Rogers or Dave Ramsey: *"You'll stop buying things you don't need with money you don't have to impress people you don't like."* You'll realize that possessions don't equal joy and that pretty often, it's pretty much the opposite. Plus, often simply maintaining your possessions will drain your money.

So, once you get rid of unnecessary possessions and don't spend any more on acquiring new ones, you will have money to spend on things that are much more valuable like experiences.

You might even rid yourself of debt. I was debt free for most of my life, and it was great. Even when I started my business, I only took a $20000 loan and the rate was pretty low. I always rented apartment and houses so I never had the feeling of being late with the mortgage. That's probably why I sleep so amazingly well.

When this book goes into print, I'll be debt free. I still know what it feels like to have a $200,000 mortgage and be struggling every month as I saw it happening to my parents. (That's probably the reason I never wanted to buy a house.)

Another advantage is that whatever happens in these strange times we live in, I'll never feel like I lost everything as long as I can take my one suitcase with me.

Last but not least, by adopting Minimalism, you will do something good for our planet—as excessive consumerism is the root cause or at least one of the root causes of our world's problems.

When you choose to live with less, you're contributing to a better future for our planet. But as I said in the introduction this should still be a personal choice and not be forced on you by psychopath billionaires and corrupt politicians (who will get richer in the process).

TRACK YOUR INCOME AND EXPENSES

You've seen that minimalism has lots of financial benefits, and while it's a great first step, it won't automatically and magically fix all your financial problems. It needs a little more than that.

Something that helped me enormously was tracking my income and expenses. And while income looked pretty bad just five years ago, it looks pretty awesome now. If you want to change any situation, you need to take a hard look at it. That's what I did. Money was draining out, so I thought I might have a closer look at it so that at least I know where it goes.

Tracking your income and expenses will give you an exact overview of your situation and is the first step to healthy finances.

What's your net income, and what (and where) are you spending your money on?

What are variable monthly costs, and what are fixed monthly costs

Monthly expenses are, for example:

- Mortgage or Rent
- Groceries
- Fuel
- Insurances
- Savings for retirement
- Gas / electricity / utilities / Water
- Loans
- Cable
- Phone
- Internet
- Cell phone
- Entertainment
- Restaurants
- Transport

This plan shows you your financial situation, and you should be able to find patterns and opportunities to cut costs.

Now you are in charge. I still recommend not to concentrate too much on only the money that's going out (you attract/see more of what you concentrate on)

Two crazy things happened to me when I started tracking my income and expenses.

1. When I summed up my daily expenses every day, I started becoming obsessed with spending "Oh no, I already spent $500 and it's only the 10th!)—so exactly what I mentioned above was happening. I was concentrated so much on money going out that even more money was going out. So, I decided to track daily but only to sum up at the end of the month. That worked.
2. Even crazier: I named my Excel sheet "Expenses 2017" and I was struggling all the time. Then I remembered

the power of words (and the subconscious mind) and renamed the Excel sheet "Income and Expenses"—it might be a coincidence, but since then my income has grown a lot, and my expenses have gone down considerably. As I said, you attract/see more of what you concentrate on.

It might take some time, but many financial experts say that controlling and tracking your income and expenses is the first step toward bringing more abundance and money into your life.

I'd say it's worth a try!

13

WHAT'S UNCLUTTERING?

Everything that you do not use or need has to go. Period. The fun thing is as soon as you start removing clutter, you are making room for new things (better stuff, experiences, friends) to come in. It's magic. It seems like the universe is saying: "Oh. Mary is taking care of her things now, getting rid of the things she doesn't need. Let's give her some new, better, more useful stuff."

Uncluttering is about letting go. But not just letting go of things. It's also letting go of the fear that keeps you holding on to stuff that you don't need anymore.
It's all about energy. If you have too much stuff that you don't use in your house, it drains your energy. Clutter is stuck energy, and it accumulates.

So, what is clutter anyway? As I mentioned above, everything you don't use is clutter. Add to this things that are unorganized, things you don't love, and even anything that's unfinished.

My journey to minimalism and uncluttering started with cleaning my cupboard. Once you are done with the cupboard, take on the whole bedroom. Later move on to the bathroom, living room, clean out your garage, and end up cleaning up your entire home and office. Get rid of everything that you don't use anymore: clothes, journals, books, CDs, even furniture, and so on. It will be amazing. I'll tell you more about it in the next chapters.

Why did you avoid uncluttering so far? Probably because it's pretty overwhelming. I also had various failed attempts before I succeeded. When you start uncluttering, various uncomfortable emotions come up so instead of facing them, we rather postpone. But that's not a solution. Not facing emotions never is.

The most common emotions are

- Regret *(Why the heck did I buy this? I'm never wearing it)*
- Fear *(What if I need this one day?*—see above*)*
- And Guilt. *(Mom / Uncle Jack / My friend Tom gave me this. I can't throw this away.)*

Guilt and Fear are definitely the most difficult emotions to handle. That's why I find Marie Kondo's approach fantastic. With her KonMari Method, you start your uncluttering process with clothes. Then linens, towels, etc. Once you come to the heavily emotionally charged items like gifts, photos, or cards, you are an expert in decision making because you have made hundreds of decisions about what stays and what goes. By then, it will be a lot easier to decide about the emotionally charged things.

When I unclutter, I usually give stuff away for free. It just makes me feel better, and somehow, I think life/God/the universe will reward me for it.

One of my clients uncluttered his whole apartment in one week-end. He felt so much better and lighter and got an energy boost that helped him to finish a whole bunch of his short-term goals. He never looked back. You can read his story in his own words in the next chapter. Originally it appeared as Chapter 31 of my book, *30 DAYS—Change your habits, change your life.*

One amazing thing that happened to me after uncluttering physical stuff is that I was on such a streak that I started uncluttering non-physical clutter from my life: unnecessary painful emotions, bad relationships, bad business partners. It was incredible. And still today, I can point to the exact month that was one of the decisive ones for the start of my success. December 2017. I got rid of three toxic business relationships that caused me many problems (bad payers and bad clients). From then on, everything changed. Four months later, I discovered a way to sell far more books and the rest is history.

Once you unclutter, the energy starts flowing again.
Once you have done your first purge, your first uncluttering, the challenge is to keep your space uncluttered. Clutter will start piling again, but it will be easier for you if you observe where. For me, it's the dining room table (which is also the home office desk), the living room table, the kitchen counter, the bathroom countertop, and bedroom dressers.

Clutter builds up slowly. Usually, you don't notice it until it's too late. Mostly, it builds on surfaces and then attracts more clutter so I keep these surfaces clean. There are some surfaces that need daily attention. Make it a daily habit to keep these surfaces clean, to hang your coat when you come in, to keep your countertop clean of mail and coins. Find a space for your keys and put them there every single time. I also purge my clothes regularly—every three months or so. Just in case.

So, the BIG question is . . . When will you start uncluttering?

Action Step:
Schedule a weekend and get rid of everything you don't need anymore! **SCHEDULE THE WEEKEND NOW!**

14

HOW TO START UNCLUTTERING? GO FOR SMALL WINS!

Once you start your minimalism adventure, you go at it like at everything else. Small steps. One after another until you succeed.

You don't have to unclutter your whole house in one weekend—although I've heard of people who did it. But most of us mortals would be so overwhelmed by the task that we don't even start. So, start small. Start with the smallest possible way that is still manageable for you. Your cupboard? Overwhelmed? Start with your T-shirts, or socks, or underwear but START!

Then for tomorrow, set another small goal and another and another. You'll find a great ally in the process. MOMENTUM. Success breeds success. Victory leads to victory. And your small everyday wins will fuel you and finally sum up to an even bigger win.

Minimalism breeds more minimalism. Once your cupboard is decluttered, you will feel freer and lighter, so you will probably tackle the next project. Maybe the bathroom.

Start with the smallest possible decluttering project, gain confidence, feel the joy and go from there.

This is the order I went: Cupboard, Bedroom, Bathroom, Guest room, Kitchen, Living room, Patio.

Change at your own convenience, having the above in mind. I chose the rooms with the least amount of clutter first. And I think I attacked the cupboard two or three times until I found the heart to get rid of all the unnecessary stuff.

So, let's get to the process of uncluttering. As I mentioned before, I followed Mari Kondo's system.

She insists on touching every item and ask yourself, "Does it spark joy?" and if it doesn't—out it goes.

So, I made a big mountain of my clothes and started the show. After some time, I had two mountains. Clothes to be kept and clothes to be discarded. In this case that meant donated, but it can also mean sold, recycled, or thrown away.

More to come in the next chapter . .

.

15

HOW TO UNCLUTTER

If you buy ten books on minimalism, you get ten systems on "how to unclutter." Most of them with a fancy name on it or the name of the "Inventor," but in the end they are all the same just written or explained a bit differently.

So, the "Marc Reklau Super Duper Method For Uncluttering Your House" is actually based on Marie Kondo's KonMari method because that was the first book I read on uncluttering (I didn't know then that it would make me a Minimalist, I just wanted to feel the *Magic of Tidying Up*). It contains traces of other methods like those from Steve Scott and Barrie Davenport, Joshua Becker, The Minimalists, and Olivia Telford. It also doesn't really have this stupid name, and it's also not rocket science, and that's why I won't write twenty pages explaining to you how to clean your house.

I will tell you what helped me, though: First of all, you'll need to make time. If you want to learn more about making time, I've also written a whole book on Time Management.
Did you schedule a weekend in your calendar as I asked you two chapters ago?

Then you need supplies. Some people will give you long lists, including cardboard boxes, permanent markers, etc. This is not the place. I used trash bags. That's it.

I told you the force of the minimalist is strong with this one. (If you want long lists and somebody to tell you how to clean your house, I'll put some recommended reading at the end of the book, but it's really not rocket science.)

Okay. Back to the "Marc Reklau Super Duper Method For Uncluttering Your House."

Start with the cupboard. Go from cupboard to cupboard, drawer to drawer, room to room. Actually, you should start with what comes easiest to you to gain some momentum. For me, that was the cupboard.

Start with clothes. Letters and gifts and all highly emotionally charged items should be set aside. It's very hard to get rid of these items in the beginning. That's why they should come last because by then, you'll already be used to making tough decisions.

I'm not going to tell you how many books you should keep. Mari Kondo says 15. If you follow her, you can only keep three books apart from all the books I wrote. Ha-ha. Just kidding. You decide. I found a great way. I threw away half of my books. The other half is in my better half Natalia's flat where they don't take away space in my suitcase.

Decluttering is really overwhelming. That's why I started with one drawer of my cupboard. Then another one. Then another one. I literally threw all my clothes on the floor and started sorting. Remember the key phrases that meant direct discarding of the item:

- "This will be useful one day."

- "Maybe I'll need this one day."
- "This reminds me of good times."

Clothes that you haven't worn for one to one and a half years or more should go

And yes, I really asked, "**Does it spark joy?**" and when it didn't—out it went.

If you're keeping stuff that doesn't fit anymore because you're planning to lose weight to wear them again . . . Throw them away. It rarely happens. I got rid of a lot of clothes following this rule. I had three pairs of unworn jeans hanging in my cupboard for three years until I finally found the strength to give them away.

You don't have to throw everything out in the first round. I did about three rounds until I threw things out that could have gone in round one.

So, after the cupboard I'd to towels and linen. Don't forget to always empty the space. And put all the contents on the floor.

Uncluttering is getting rid of stuff. Not reorganizing stuff. Not shifting stuff from one place to another. Stuff has to GO.

I actually made a checklist. I think it was inspired by Steve Scott and Barrie Davenport:

- purge clothes closet. (Does it spark joy?)
- Purge linen, towels, bed sheets
- Clean out shower
- Purge bathroom cabinets
- Clean off the kitchen table
- Clear off kitchen counters

- Purge 2 kitchen cabinets
- Organize cleaning supplies
- Clean out fridge
- Purge two more kitchen cabinets
- Clean out freezer
- Purge more kitchen cabinets
- Go through paperwork
- Discard old books (Remove all books from shelves and ask, "Does it spark joy?")
- Get rid of extra accessories
- Papers, Study materials, Online seminars, Business cards, instruction manuals, Greeting cards, birthday cards, pens that don't work (Rule of thumb: **Discard everything)**
- **Miscellaneous:** CDs, DVDs, Valuables, electric equipment, cables, household supplies, samples, kitchen goods, small change, gifts
- Clean, discard, decide where to put things, and decide what you want to keep.

Other rules:

- Discard first, store later
- Storage: ultimate simplicity
- Don't scatter storage spaces
- Clutter is caused by failure to return things where they belong
- Put bags into another bag (no more than two)

Things you no longer use are clutter. This includes all kinds of equipment like the old stereo you don't use anymore, fitness equipment you bought and never used, car accessories, sports equipment, garden equipment, and so on (yes, you can probably throw out / sell 80% of the stuff in your garage)

16

UNCLUTTERING AND TOLERATIONS GO HAND IN HAND – A REAL LIFE EXAMPLE

This is a chapter from my book *30 DAYS*. It describes the experience of my client Lawrence who describes what happened when he started uncluttering and tackling his tolerations.

"When I went through the process of uncluttering my life, it was like I was creating a new sense of freedom for myself. Before I understood what cluttering is, I had been going through life picking up so many bad habits and discouraging thoughts along the way . . . They weren't the type of habits like a vice, for example, smoking or drinking. They were more like small tolerations that were seemingly insignificant to begin with, but as I gained more and more of them in my life and just accepted them as something I couldn't change, they grew heavier until I was very weighed down.

These tolerations made me feel like I was moving like a sloth. Things like procrastination, lack of sleep, not gaining fulfillment from my work, getting used to take-out food too often, beating myself up for not achieving more success . . . Somewhere along the way I lost sight of my goals in life and I just allowed these tolerations to clutter things up to the point that I felt stuck.

When my coach Marc introduced the idea of uncluttering to me, it was truly a revelation. I understood what it meant immediately, but I just didn't know why I was this way or how to fix it and climb out of the hole. With the tools that Marc helped to equip me with, I can now recognize my tolerations and work on unloading them.

I've identified the ones that I could quickly fix and have gotten rid of them: fixing the window sill that wouldn't open, hanging up the paintings that I left in storage when I moved, replacing my old mattress that was not so comfortable.

I also recognize the tolerations that will take more time to resolve, and I work on them all the time, like challenging myself more at work and getting gratification from that productivity. I've written down all of them to keep track of and to hold myself accountable, and I write down new tolerations as I identify them along the way.

Uncluttering the tolerations in my life, that were jumbled together in my mind and slowing me down, has made me feel like I am 10x lighter now. I have more energy, more spirit, and more enthusiasm. And as I uncluttered the tolerations, I found that my physical surroundings became uncluttered as well. My apartment is cleaner and more open, so I feel like I'm in a clutter-free environment at home."

17

STAY CLUTTER-FREE

If you think uncluttering is hard, wait until you see how hard it is to stay clutter-free. All this newfound space, the universe wants to fill again.

So how to stay clutter-free?

- Have a place for everything and return everything to its place.
- Get organized. This means store similar things together, keep things near where you're going to use them, put the things you use most often in the places that are easiest to reach.
- I use the KonMari Method for my cupboard, so I organized my wardrobe according to color. It looks great. I hope it's not the beginning of obsessive-compulsive disorder.
- Think twice before your buy
- When something new comes in, something old goes out.
- Let go of attachment and throw away things. You'll get better at it the more often you repeat the uncluttering process.

- Clutter builds up slowly mostly without you even noticing it so purge regularly. Evaluate stuff regularly to see if it's still necessary or if it has become clutter.
- Go through your wardrobe every six to twelve months (maybe even every three to six months) and make sure something old goes out before something new comes in.
- Stop the inward flow of things.
- Limit your shopping trips, think before you buy, and keep track of what you really need.
- When you need something that you think is really necessary, don't buy it right away. Write it down and wait a couple of days—sometimes even seven to fourteen—and then see if you still want or need it.

18

WHEN SOMETHING COMES IN, SOMETHING HAS TO GO OUT

Whenever something new comes in, something old has to go out. Once you have decluttered your home, you want to keep it that way. And to keep it that way, you have to adhere to the mentioned rule because if not, your home is going to get cluttered quickly again.

It's amazing and some kind of magic. You can try this at home. Whenever you want something new to enter your life, make room in your cupboard, in your house, in your garage. It seems like the universe wants to fill empty spaces.

Whenever I felt stuck in the last few years (when I still had a lot of stuff), I did a round of uncluttering. I could be sure something new entered my life. New ideas, new inspiration, new people, new opportunities. I don't think those were coincidences. I mean how big of a coincidence can it be if it happens every friggin' single time?

And I see it in other people, too. A friend of mine, let's call her Nadia, was doing okay in her business, but she wanted more and more didn't come. Then suddenly—probably subconsciously—she got this urge to declutter. Her place was really very cluttered.

So, she got rid of half the stuff she had. Many things just being there "in case she needs them one day." Now her telephone doesn't stop. I can understand you when you think this is baloney, and I'm not offended. I'd probably think so too if I hadn't experienced the magic of uncluttering so many times.

By the way, did I tell you that I'm down to 18 T-shirts now and regularly wearing the same seven to eight all the time? I just threw two out that didn't "spark joy" anymore. I also have three pairs of jeans. Eighty percent of the time, I'm wearing the same pair.

Anyways. If you have a lot of things and want to create space for the universe to fill, you have to throw something out first. If you already don't have a lot of stuff, you can also do it the other way round. Something new comes in. Let's say two pairs of jeans, two T-shirts, and a sweater come in, then two old jeans, two old T-shirts, and an old sweater have to go. If I buy new shoes, one pair of shoes goes. Right now, I have achieved something no woman can ever achieve. I only own **three** pairs of shoes (and one in Natalia's flat). And of course, women could achieve that, but you don't have to. As I said at the beginning, adopt your own style of minimalism.

Of course, this goes for dishes, linen, pots, etc. too. But as I don't own any of those, I always come up with examples that include clothes. I remember how on my boat there were twenty pillows that came with it. Guess how many I kept: six.

You need to stop the inward flow of stuff. If not, your place will be cluttered again in no time. So there should actually always be less coming in than going out.
Make a commitment to never ever buy anything again that you're not 100% sure that you will wear or use it. If you think "I might use it someday"—Don't buy it. If you think "This might be

useful," don't buy it. Buy only things that you love. If you have to ask, "Does this look good on me?" Don't buy it.

Think before you buy. As t told you before, it's not much fun being at a mall with me. I already know what I NEED. Then I check all the shops once and take mental notes of what I'd like to buy—but don't buy anything the first time around. Then I take the second round and notice that I don't need 95% of the stuff that I thought I wanted to buy. Most of the time, when I "go shopping" at a mall, I come home empty-handed. Boring? Yes! But that's why I live in a clutter-free and minimalist environment.

Never go shopping when you are emotionally drained. It's the same as going to the supermarket when you are hungry . . . You buy a lot of stuff that you don't even like.

If you think you really, really need something, don't purchase it immediately. Instead, write it down. If you still want to buy it after a week or two, then go buy it.

19

QUALITY INSTEAD OF QUANTITY

Once I got rid of most of the stuff I didn't need, I made a commitment to myself (inspired by Joshua Becker's book *Simplify*) to buy less stuff but better quality stuff. So instead of having 40 (!!) T-shirts, I bought 10 great quality T-shirts that I really like. I still notice that I always wear the same five, six T-shirts, so there is room for improvement.

I now apply this to everything. When I need to buy something, I buy high-quality stuff. Cheap is expensive because cheap is usually not that durable. If you buy low-quality stuff, you'll find yourself back in the store a couple of months later because low-quality stuff just doesn't last.

I only own three pairs of jeans (but they are great jeans) and around five sweaters. If you live in a cold country, you might need more sweaters or maybe not. I live in Hungary now, which is pretty cold in winter so I thought I'd better buy some sweaters. I noticed I didn't need one. My winter jacket is of such great quality that I can wear only a T-shirt with it and not freeze. Guess how many winter jackets I own? Right. Two. I also have a dryer (Yes. You guessed it: it came with the flat). That helps when

I have to wash my super winter jacket. Two hours and I can go back out in the cold.

You can apply quality over quantity to everything in your life. Kitchen things, furniture, linen, towels, even people! I have few friends but high-quality friends. In the end, life is too short to live with mediocrity.

Choose quality over quantity in every area of your life.

20

IT'S JUST STUFF

I don't have a lot of stuff.
I have three pairs of shoes and three pairs of flip-flops. Three pairs of jeans. (You know that by now…)

When you look at what you're wearing, aren't you always wearing your five favorite shirts? Your three favorite sweaters, your six favorite T-shirts?
Once I noticed that, I got rid of a lot of stuff.

When I tell you that all my stuff fits into one suitcase, that comes with a price. In the last five years, I have bought three coffee machines, two toasters, two grills, two TVs, two projectors, and two cold press juicers, which in the end I gave away. For me, that's okay. A small price to pay for having peace of mind.

Why do I only own three pairs of shoes? Because I'm only wearing two of them most of the time anyway.

Having less stuff also means you know where to find everything.

I remember when I moved from my house to my boat. I found six boxes that were untouched since my last move. I hadn't touched these boxes for six years. I figured there was nothing important in there. I still opened them, and then I threw 90% of their contents away. If I hadn't missed the contents for six years, they can't have been that important—and they weren't.

Okay. This might be hard, but I'm going to put it out there. Most of the things you have are just stuff. Yup. No matter how important you think these things are . . . they are just stuff. Ninety percent of this stuff you won't even miss. That doesn't mean that you have to get rid of it now. Observe. If you didn't touch it for two or three years, it's probably just stuff and can go.

Having fewer things will also mean having fewer things to worry about. Remember the saying, "What you own, owns you." Well, the less you own, the less owns you. And remember, "the last shirt doesn't have any pockets"—meaning you won't be able to take anything with you once you're not here anymore. So instead of having too much stuff and worrying about what to do with it (Who will get your stamp or thimble collection), get rid of it in your life and spend the remaining time with your loved ones, laughing with friends, walking in nature or reading awesome books.
Downsize now, and remember it's just stuff.

21

ELIMINATE EVERYTHING THAT ANNOYS YOU

Everything that annoys you drains your energy. In coaching, we call this "tolerations." Tolerations are the little things you might not even notice but which drain you of energy.

Once you hone in on them, you might 50 to 100 things. No worries. It's normal.
This can be a light bulb that needs changing, a missing button on your favorite shirt, a dirty shower curtain, a dent in your car, a disorganized guest room, a drawer full of unnecessary stuff, broken tools, a messy desk, clothes that don't fit anymore.

All these are tolerations, and they drain your energy even if you don't notice it.
Anything unfinished is also a toleration, so finish your unfinished business. That includes emails you have to write, phone calls you have to make, and even relationships you need to finish

Once you start uncluttering, many tolerations will go. This will liberate more and more energy and bring more and more clarity into your life.

Your turn:

- Make a list of all the things that annoy you in your house and your job, and don't get scared if you write down 50 to 100 things. It's normal.
- Once you have written everything down, group them:
- Which ones are easy to handle? Which ones can YOU handle? For now, leave the ones that don't depend on you.

I've seen many times that some of the tolerations that don't depend on you disappear on their own once you take care of the ones that you can handle. It's miraculous.

Start making that list! Do it NOW!

22

TIE UP LOOSE ENDS

When you clear unsolved issues that you have in your life and tie up loose ends, magic happens. It seems like while there is unfinished business, it's more difficult for new, better things to come into your life. Lots of energy is tied down, lots of space in your mind occupied—even though sometimes you don't notice it. Unfinished business weighs you down.

Tying up loose ends also is a part of decluttering and minimizing that has to be brought in order.

So, pay back any money you owe, return any items you have borrowed, forgive the people you have forgiven, and ask for forgiveness where due. I know. It's difficult. It's also worth it.

Do what you've said you'll do. Every unfulfilled promise, every commitment you make and don't fulfill drains your energy and has a psychological effect on you. Don't make promises you can't keep. Don't take commitments you can't keep. If you always say yes to everything without thinking and then regret it later, make a rule for yourself to never answer right away when someone asks you to commit, attend an event, or do them a favor. Buy time. Say, "I'll look into it and tell you later." Once you have thought about it, you can give the answer.

Words are powerful. The problem is when you break your word too many times, not only others won't trust you anymore—even worse—you won't trust yourself anymore because with every broken promise and unattended commitment, you're telling yourself: "My word has no worth. Thus, as a consequence, I myself am worthless."

Don't let it come to this extreme. Be aware of the value of your word and act accordingly.

23

GET RID OF ENERGY ROBBERS

One fantastic side effect of uncluttering is that you get rid of a lot of energy robbers that you probably didn't even know you had.

Your energy is crucial for boosting you towards your goals, clarity, and happiness.

There are some things in your life that drain your energy, and there are things that add energy. Don't underestimate the importance of energy and keep it up!

When you operate on low energy, you don't feel good, you are not happy, you send out low vibes, and chances are that you will attract what you are sending.

We know the typical energy drains like unhealthy eating habits, alcohol, drugs, caffeine, sugar, tobacco, lack of exercise, negativity, sarcasm, unfocused goals, the news, tabloid newspapers, and **even people,** among others, but did you know that too much stuff also drains your energy? And a lot!

This is another reason why uncluttering and being a minimalist are so magical. Energy drains are gotten rid of. The process of uncluttering includes eliminating distractions, finishing unfinished business, eliminating tolerations, and saying goodbye to all energy robbing people and relationships.

24

STOP SPENDING TIME WITH THE WRONG PEOPLE!

One of the biggest surprises of my becoming a minimalist is that when I started decluttering my life of things I didn't need or that didn't spark joy, when I had gone through my cupboards and all the rooms of my house, it didn't stop there.

I started uncluttering my relationships. This was an urge. It's also about energy. Emotions and attitudes are contagious. People around you can be the springboard to motivate yourself, gain courage, and help you take the right actions, but on the other hand can also drag you down, drain your energy, manipulate you, and act as brakes in achieving of your life goals. Sometimes hanging out with this kind of friend might even throw a bad light on your reputation (birds of the same feather . . .).

Choose wisely who you hang out with. Spend time with people who bring out the best in you, who motivate you, who believe in you. Be around people who empower you. It will be difficult for you to grow and thrive if the people around you want to convince you of the contrary.

This also goes for business relationships, and it's amazing what happened when I uncluttered my business relationships. At the time I was finished with uncluttering "stuff," I had the urge to look at my relationships. Three business relationships stood out. They brought in 25% of my revenue, but when I analyzed them it looked ugly. They were really toxic.

One was only bad news and problems every time they called, and the other two were bad payers always paying very late. Always having new excuses as to why they couldn't pay on time. So, I decided to end the relationship politely and thought, "Uh uh, Marc. I guess you'll make 25% less next year."

You won't believe what happened next . . . or maybe you saw it coming. At the end of the year, I didn't have 25% less. I had 15% more. Looking back, it seems logical. I had a lot more space (in my brain and my life), and instead of going after my money or solving problems of complicated customers, I used my time to get creative, write more, and make more money.

It's no coincidence that just three months after ending these relationships, I laid the foundation of my success today. The more I think about it, the clearer it gets. If I had to pinpoint where and when my success started that enabled me to live my dream life today, I would point you to when I started with minimalism but mainly when I got rid of those three business relationships. This was clearly the turning point, and if you want to see it metaphysically through my actions, "getting rid of something that holds me back," I showed the universe / god / all that is "I'm ready. I'm taking a risk. I'm going in the right direction. Send more of the good in my direction."

I've seen the same thing happening to many people since. Clean up your relationships, and good things will happen.

And what do you do if it is people close to you? The only thing you can work on is becoming a better person yourself. If you grow and develop, soon negative people will turn away from you because you don't serve their purposes anymore. They need somebody who shares their negativity and if you don't do that, they will look for somebody else. If that doesn't work, you seriously have to ask yourself the question if you should start to spend less time with them or stop seeing them at all. **But that's a decision you have to make.**

Action Steps:

1. Make a list of all the people you have in your life and are spending time with (members of your family, friends, colleagues).
2. Analyze who is positive for you and who drags you down.
3. Spend more time with the positive people and stop seeing the toxic people (blamers, complainers) in your life, or at least spend less time with them.
4. Choose to be around positive people who support you.

25

STOP CRITICIZING

When we're talking about decluttering everything, we have to talk about decluttering your mind. I don't want to go too deep into it, but we should look at some bad habits that are best to avoid and one of them is the bad and totally useless habit of criticizing.

I shouldn't be the one to write it because I don't like to be criticized at all—even if the critique comes dressed as "constructive."

The thought that criticism can improve something is old and outdated. Criticism only brings resentment and can demoralize family members, friends, colleagues, and employees. It's dangerous because it hurts our pride and puts us on the defensive.

Additionally, criticism usually comes from people that haven't achieved anything. Only mediocre people have time to criticize their peers. Successful people are usually too busy being successful and have no time for nitpicking.

Last but not least, it's proven that we learn more, become better, and are more productive when our good behavior is praised and acknowledged than if we get punished and work under pressure.

A critical comment just before an important presentation in the likes of "Pete, this is very important for us. Don't screw it up like last time" can set the person up for failure while encouraging and praising the strengths of a person like "John, I admire how you prepare these presentations. Go and knock it out of the park" can seal the deal.

Don't misunderstand me. I happily accept criticism from people who are more successful and have achieved what I want to achieve. Funnily enough, those people never criticize! They only empower you. Only small minds criticize because they are either cowards or too weak to create something themselves, or both.

Stop trying to change people and start by changing yourself. Be the change you want to see in others—be the role model, be the example.

No good will come out of criticizing others. Swallow your criticism and work on yourself instead.

26

STOP GOSSIPING

Another useless habit that will only cost you energy and probably even friends is the toxic habit of gossiping.

Stay away from gossip and rumors as they are only harmful and destructive. I know, sometimes it's very tempting to hear the latest rumors from other people. I must be. Whole entertainment and TV programs are built on it. Following gossip also keeps you from working and becoming successful.

Once again—I know I repeat myself like a broken record—successful people don't waste energy and time on gossiping. They have more important things to do.

More often than not, the person who tells you these rumors is probably also talking back about you behind your back. I'm sure you have people like this in your environment—if not, congratulations. But usually there's always this person. The one that if you want a rumor to spread like wildfire you only have to tell it to that person and ask them to keep it a secret and not to say a word on it. Bam. It'll spread like wildfire.

What is even worse for your reputation is what happens if you are the one spreading the dirty little stories. What if your listeners come to the same logical conclusion I mentioned above.

The worst thing that can happen to you is that they start asking themselves what you say about them behind their backs once they turn them to YOU.

The best thing is not to enter the vicious circle of gossiping. You do that by changing the subject or simply stating: "Sorry, I really don't like talking about people who aren't present."

Don't damage your trustworthiness and relationships by gossiping. Have sincere and profound conversations as they are a lot more empowering and beneficial.

Stop gossiping. Be a person of integrity.

27

STOP COMPARING

The quickest way to misery and unhappiness is to constantly compare yourself to other people. That's why social media makes us feel miserable.

Yes, it even happens to me. There's always someone who has more or is more successful. Somebody who has more money, a nicer car, a better six-pack, a bigger office, a book that sells more, etc. Accept it and move on. Comparing yourself to others is a completely useless habit. It makes no sense. When you compare yourself to others, you'll feel either superior or inferior, and neither one is true. You are you. Period.

This also goes for minimalism. Don't compare your minimalism to other people's way of minimalism. It's not possible. You have to do what's best for you. It's your journey.

It's sounds like one of these motivational phrases on social media —that's because it is one—but that doesn't make it less true: **The only person you should be in competition with is the person you were yesterday.**

Focus on yourself. Focus on what you can do to become a better you. Focus on your strengths and build them. When envy (this sneaky MF) sneaks into my mind—yes, it even happens to me—for example, envying the success of someone, I directly reframe the envy into admiration and ask myself how can I become as successful as this person. What do they do?

Use people that have what you don't have as a source of inspiration instead of envying them.

If you really have a hard time working on this one, maybe you should get off social media for a while.

Studies suggest that social media plays a major part in the creation of jealousy and envy because we watch other people's highlight reel and compare it to our "behind the scenes" movie and that just can't work.

If you go to my Facebook page, you'll see pictures of me working at the beach, having a coffee on the beach, traveling to nice places. But don't get fooled. That's only a snapshot of half an hour or an hour of my day. The other ten hours, I'm locked up at home working.

I also don't post my failures. Maybe I should. You can't imagine how many times I was rejected, ridiculed, or just treated badly. It doesn't matter. What's important is what we do with these experiences.

Do yourself a favor. Don't compare yourself to others.

28

STOP COMPLAINING

As we keep on throwing out mental trash, this one is one of the first things that has to go. The bad habit of complaining. Complaining is an absolutely useless behavior that doesn't accomplish anything except encouraging self-pity and making you a less likable person. I hate to bring it to you, but who wants to spend time with a complainer. Yes. Exactly. No one. Except for other complainers, maybe. Complainers are not attractive at all. It's a victim's mentality, and that isn't you because you're taking life into your hands.

If complaining was any good and accomplished anything, I'd encourage you to do it. But it's not.
Personally, I stick to Lou Holtz's rule, "Never tell your problems to anyone . . . 20% don't care and the other 80% are glad you have them."

And I admit, I complain every now and then just to blow off some steam. Nobody is perfect. But then I get a grip and remember what I'm writing in my books and then I fix it.

If I don't have time, I have to go find it.

If my book is not well received, I have to go back to the drawing board and improve it.

I don't blame my parents, teachers, ex-girlfriends, ex-bosses, the government or the economy for my life. I learn how to improve it, perhaps by reading a book (or ten) for example.

If I'm not happy with my weight, I have to options: complain and do nothing or exercise. Or a third one. Do nothing but at least don't complain.

So, stop complaining. It's nobody's fault but your own that you go on smoking, eat unhealthy food, or give up on your dreams. It's you who pushes the snooze button instead of getting up half an hour earlier and who chooses fear over risk. Don't blame others for not living a satisfying life. You own your life! You can do anything you want with it. The sooner you get this, the sooner you can move on in the direction of your dreams.

Remember where to keep your focus! Complaining about your present circumstances will put your focus on them and "attract" more of what you don't like. You have to get out of this vicious circle and concentrate on what you want instead

Look inside yourself and encourage your positive ambitions and will to succeed. Now go and create the circumstances you want. Start making decisions and start living.

Action Steps:

- Make a list of all your complaints.
- Analyze: What have your complaints achieved?
- In writing: Transform your complaints into requests.

29

STOP WORRYING

Many years ago, I was a big worrier. It was horrible. I was always worrying. Worrying about things that happened in the past that I couldn't change, things in the future that I had no influence over, or about economy, wars, and politics that I had no control over.

Even funnier is that most of the catastrophes that I was worrying about turned out to be a lot less horrible in reality than in my imagination or just never happened.

Everything changed the day I stepped on a plane whose engine exploded in midair ten or fifteen minutes after taking off. Like on so many days, I had worried about thousands of things on that day—one of the few things I hadn't worried about was the engine of my plane exploding midair.

This was one of the worst experiences of my life and at the same time one of the best ones. I walked away from it with a huge fear of flying that developed in the months after. But I also walked away more authentic, more clear, more me, and with a different perspective on life—and a lot less of a worrier.

I enjoyed life a lot more after that experience as I saw how quickly it could end. I know . . . my engineer friends told me a plane can fly with two engines without any problems and that only one in a hundred planes with an exploded engine crash. The problem is that everybody on that plane thought that we were on the one that would crash.

My favorite phrase in danger of falling back into old *worrying behavior is this one from the Dalai Lama: "If a problem is fixable, if a situation is such that you can do something about it, then there is no need to worry. If it's not fixable, then there is no help in worrying. There is no benefit in worrying whatsoever."* So simple. So powerful.

I also like to think of Mark Twain, who said, "I've had a lot of worries in my life, most of which never happened."

It doesn't matter how much you worry; it will change neither the past not the future! Also, worrying usually doesn't make things any better, does it? Instead, it will drag you down and you will lose the present moment.

One more thing you can do if you are a big worrier is to make a list of your worries. Cross out the ones related to your past that can't be changed. Then you cross out the ones related to the future that will probably never happen. Then cross out the ones that are not in your control.

Now you are left with the ones that are in your control. I'd guess that's only 5% to 15% of the worries that you had before this little exercise. You should have gotten rid of 85% to 95% of your worries, right?
Yes. Identifying your worries and dropping the ones that you can't do anything about and which only were draining your energy you probably eliminated 85% to 95% of your worries (I bet it's closer to 95%).

Try this at home and try it NOW:

Action step:

- Make a list of your worries:

Questions:

- Which ones are related to the past?
- Which ones are related to the future?
- Which ones are outside your control?
- Which ones can you actually do something about?

30

STOP JUDGING

Another habit that will do no good for you is the toxic habit of judging other people. Once again, it's a habit that has no real benefit at all for you—except the one that makes you feel better about your own life that's probably not the way you want it.

Have you ever noticed that happy and successful people with a great life don't judge and don't care about other people's lives unless they can contribute something beneficial to it? Let that sink in.

It's difficult not to get tempted to judge other people because we'd love that everybody was just like us and would do the things that we want them to do. It won't happen, so you might as well substitute this bad habit with another one that's actually good for you, like reading or learning more.

Sometimes when something bothers us about people, we need to look at ourselves because we might be doing those things to others without noticing it. That's why you have people whose life is in disarray telling you how you should live your life; people with a ton of debt telling you how to deal with your finances; overweight people telling you to eat healthier; unorganized and stressed people giving seminars for time management and organization and so on.

If you don't like things about other people and are tempted to point those out, look at yourself first. Are these maybe things that bother you about yourself? Every time you're judging someone, you're actually judging yourself. There is a great Spanish proverb: "What Juan says about Pedro, says more about Juan than it says about Pedro."

As I mentioned, it's really tough not to judge people. The temptation is always there. I really avoid judging people as I have found myself more than once in the same situations as people that I judged before. That's really scary, but it helps a lot with dealing with that toxic habit. More than once, I was in the same situation as the people I judged when I came to understand them.

There's really something to the saying "Walk a mile (or maybe better ten) in my shoes before you judge me."
Since then, whenever I'm tempted to judge someone, I think, "Uh, uh. Danger. You might find yourself in the same situation. Stop judging. Go do something positive."

Just be kind and get your own house in order before you judge others. Work on your own flaws and above all strengths instead of pointing out other people's flaws.

31

ADOPT A POSITIVE MINDSET

Believe it or not, your mindset has a huge impact of the outcomes in your life. While some people are kicked down or even broken by certain events, others see it as a sign to go at it again with even more vigor.

The beliefs that "there's something good in every bad" or "every situation has a positive part, you just have to find" have helped me to navigate the ups and downs of life and probably even saved my life.

How do you interpret events? As permanent ("Never") or as temporary ("one step closer")? What's failure for you? A catastrophe of an opportunity for success? Are you an optimist or a pessimist? Did you know that scientifically speaking, the difference between an optimist and a pessimist actually only boils down to one thing? And that thing is how you interpret events.

You're not born an optimist or pessimist. It's not a matter of genes. Optimism can be learned and learning to interpret events as optimists leads to much higher success. Optimism strengthens your biological and psychological immune system. And last, but not least . . . optimists live longer. (P.S. This doesn't automatically mean that all pessimists die young because there are more things to factor into that. It also doesn't mean that all optimists live long. If you smoke 40 cigarettes a day, being an optimist might not help a lot.)

But not everything is all happy and shiny in Optimismland. There's an important thing we have to be careful about. False optimism. False optimism sooner or later leads to disillusion, anger, and hopelessness. We need to train to become "realistic optimists." Positive thinking alone is not enough. You also have to add optimism, passion, and hard work to the success formula.

Another misconception is that too high expectations will lead to disappointment. (So, people stop dreaming and expecting the best for them) That is wrong. Rather, it is *false* expectations that lead to disappointment.
The false expectation often is that events can make us happy or unhappy. Wrong again.

Science found out that there are ups and downs around a base level of well-being. These ups and downs in life are inevitable; how you deal with them is your choice.

The good news is that you can take more risks. If instead of avoiding issues, you cope, confront things, take risks, deal with things, and go out and try, then your base level of happiness increases, and that's what it's all about.

Become an optimist. It's fun. (And read Martin Seligman's books on the subject.)

32

BE GRATEFUL

Are you grateful for what you already have, or are you always looking for the next shiny object? Wherever you are on your journey to become a minimalist or even if you don't want to become a minimalist at all, I highly recommend you to start practicing gratitude.

It's scientifically proven that practicing gratitude for three to four weeks rewires your brain to see more of the positive things around you. It will make you happier, more optimistic, more sociable. You'll sleep better and will be less prone to headaches. You will have more energy and more emotional intelligence. You'll become more forgiving, less prone to depression, and feel less anxiety.

I get emails daily about how gratitude has impacted the lives of my readers. It's truly amazing. One reader has gone from being single and moving back to his parents' house to sharing a house with friends and dating the love of his life. One of my former clients has gone from a contract that only gave her a percentage of sales to receiving a fixed contract and then tripling her salary. When people at a very low point in life ask me for advice, I explain that I can't give them any advice as I don't even know what I would do in their situation, and then I recommend them to practice gratitude because I know it helps.

Gratitude is my magic pill. It's the antidote to all the painful emotions that visit us every now and then like grief, envy, sadness, anger and so on. If you feel gratitude, you can't feel any of those other emotions. For me, gratitude has been a multiplier of my success. The more grateful I became the happier and more successful I became in consequence. Whenever I forgot about gratitude (it happens to the best of us. We are humans after all) my results started to dwindle.

So even if you don't choose to become a minimalist after reading this book, I hope you choose gratitude.

It's very easy.

Write down three things you are grateful for every day, in the morning, evening, or both. And feel the gratitude. That's it. It doesn't take more than five minutes, and it works.

Try it.

(If you want to read a whole book on gratitude . . . I wrote one. It's called *The Life-changing Power of Gratitude* and is one of my favorites.)

33

FORGIVE YOURSELF

You will never be perfect, and the best is: You don't have to be! Just take this minimalism thing one step at a time, one day at a time. I didn't become a minimalist in a month. As I mentioned before: I cleaned out my cupboard. I liked it. I didn't miss anything, so I cleaned it out a bit more. Then I noticed I felt lighter and better with less stuff—just like many years before I started accumulating stuff—so I got rid of some more stuff.

Like so many things, minimalism isn't a straight road. There will be setbacks, mess-ups, obstacles, and failures, like with so many other things in life—like success and habits, for example. The important thing is not to give up and to be nice to yourself. Don't beat yourself up when life doesn't go as planned. Talk to yourself like you would talk to a friend in the same situation and then go at it again.

Minimalism will make your life better, and the benefits are fantastic. A simple life might keep you sane in a world that seems to keep getting madder by the day. Having everything you need (not everything) will hopefully give you the same feelings it gives me: Peace, clarity, and freedom. You got this.

34

KEEP A JOURNAL

Keeping a journal is one of the smartest things you can do—minimalist or not. It's one of these things I wouldn't miss for the world. Science has come forth with amazing studies about the various advantages of journaling. It improves your focus, lowers stress, and has countless other health benefits.

A 2013 study by the Department of Psychological Medicine, University of Auckland, New Zealand, found that journaling promotes faster wound healing! The members of the journaling group healed 75% faster than their non-journaling counterparts.

Further research shows that journaling results in reduced absenteeism from work, quicker reemployment after a job loss, and higher GPAs for students. Think about it. People who wrote in their journals for as little as fifteen minutes a day healed their wounds faster, improved their immune systems, and improved their GPAs. If there were a pill for that, it would fly off the shelves!

Take a couple of minutes at the end of the day and reflect. What did you do well? What could you have done better? What made you happy today? What are you grateful for today? Journaling is amazing for getting perspective. Sometimes you might think you had a horrible day, but if you analyze it, it was just John who told you something you didn't like at 9 a.m. and the rest of the day was actually great.

Journaling will give you an extra boost of happiness, motivation, self-esteem, and insight. It has the great side effect that just before sleeping, you will be concentrating your mind on positive things, which has a beneficial effect on your sleep and your subconscious mind. Your focus is on the positive things of the day and gratitude instead of the things that didn't work well, which probably would keep you awake.

Make an effort to answer the following questions each night before sleeping and write them in your journal:

- What am I grateful for? (Write 3 -5 points)
- What 3 things have made me happy today?
- What 3 things did I do particularly well today?
- How could I have made today even better?
- What is my most important goal for tomorrow?

And don't worry if the words don't flow right away when you start this exercise. Like all other things, your journaling will get better with practice. If you are blocked and can't think of anything, just hold on for five minutes longer. Write what comes to mind without thinking, and don't judge it. Don't worry about your style or mistakes. This is your journal. Nobody else will see it. Just write! Do this every day for a month and observe the changes that take place! A regular notebook or calendar should do.

35

LET GO OF THE PAST

Every moment you spend in your past is a moment you steal from your present and future. Stop reliving your drama—don't hang onto it. **LET GO OF IT!** Only if you have the courage to let go of the old can you be open to new things entering your life.

Having too much clutter is also a sign of not being able to let go of the past. But as I mentioned before, if there's too much old there's no room for new things to come into our life. By starting to clear your clutter, you start dealing with your problems and make room for new things to come into your life.

On the mental level, letting go of the past means not wasting your time thinking of things that could or should have happened or that didn't work out as you wanted in the past. On the physical level, it means not holding on to things from the past that have no use anymore.

It doesn't make sense.

Learn from your past experiences and move on, and get rid of clutter. That's all you have to do from now on. Easy, isn't it?

Make room for new thoughts, new behavior, new things, and new relationships.

You need to let go of the past so that you are free and new things can come into your life! Let go of old baggage, finish unfinished business, and get closure with people. Complete the past so that you can be free to enjoy the present.

From now on, adopt the mindset that you will always finish your business. Don't leave anything incomplete in your relationships, work, and all other areas. Keep moving forward.

Action Step:

What is incomplete in your life? Make a list and work on it!

36

REWARD YOURSELF

A very important subject that we don't talk about enough is the concept of rewarding yourself when you get things done.

This will increase your focus and productivity and will get you motivated to start things and get them done. This works for everything—not only for creating a minimalist environment.

For example: If I work on my book from 7 to 10 a.m., I usually give myself a two-hour break to check my private Facebook account and/or watch one episode of my favorite series. I can only get this reward if I get my work done and reach my daily word count (2000 words).

Other rewards I give myself are, for example, meeting friends, taking a power nap, watching a movie or TV series, enjoying a nice bubble bath, going to one of the fantastic thermal baths in Budapest, or going to one of the over 100-year-old coffee houses.

In the context of uncluttering and minimalism, you can reward yourself for every task done, every room cleaned, every cupboard successfully purged. You'll come up with rewards. I know you will.

If you get into the habit of rewarding yourself for a job well done, life and work will get a lot more fun.

37

START

You've already read half of the book. What have you put into practice so far?

Starting is the most important part. It's also the most difficult part. Many people no matter their endeavor, stay stuck in the planning or preparation phase. It happens everywhere. Salespeople planning their calls so long but never make the call. Authors that have their whole book planned out but never getting started at writing—or never finish their manuscript. That's the danger of the planning process. It makes us think we are working towards our goals when we are often procrastinating on what we really have to do. Most important is GETTING STARTED.

The best way to start is to **Just Do It**. Now you know why I like Nike T-shirts. They are a constant reminder for me to take action.
The best way to start is to do it with one small step. Maybe unclutter one small drawer. This will give you the momentum and motivation to move to the next task.

Earlier in this book, I showed you how I started decluttering. Yes.

I started with one drawer. My T-shirts. I think I was with the cupboard for two days. Every day getting rid of some more unnecessary stuff.

You don't have to do it all at once. Getting rid of things is difficult. I gave it various shots. And it got better and better and the cupboard and later my house became emptier and emptier. By now you have learned that doing small things consistently on a daily basis can get you great results.

So, after all the planning and talking about minimalism, you need to make things happen. Without action, there will not be results.

So, by all means, **START NOW!** With one small thing. What is it going to be? And then take action consistently.

Just start with what you have and go one step at a time. Do as Martin Luther King, Jr. said, **"Take the first step in faith. You don't have to see the whole staircase; just take the first step."**

Action Step:
Start uncluttering one drawer TODAY!

38

100% RESPONSIBILITY

All change start with taking 100% responsibility for your life. That means that you are the only person responsible for your life .YOU. Not your boss, not your spouse, not your parents, not your friends, not your clients, not the economy, not the weather. YOU! I know that's scary isn't it. It's also liberating.

Before you misunderstand me. This doesn't mean you're responsible for everything that happens to you. Sometimes bad things happen to good people. You are, however, responsible for how you react to these things.

Once you stop blaming others for everything that happens in your life, everything changes.

You turn from victim of the circumstances to creator of your circumstances. You claim the power to decide how to act in the face of circumstances that life presents to you. You shift from the outside (the others have to change so that I can be well) to the inside (I decide how something affects me with my attitude).

Change what you can change and accept what you can't change and make the best of it. Your life is yours, and that's the biggest gift of all. You have the power to change the things that you don't like in your life. You are in control. The worst thing that will happen is that you have no one to blame anymore.

Life happens, but you are free to change your behavior. Your success in almost any endeavor depends on you. Always focus on solutions, not excuses. Act where you have control and accept where you don't have it. And yes. Life is not fair. Get used to it. It's easier to handle when you know you're in control.

So once again: Even if you don't have control over the stimuli that the environment sends, you have the liberty to choose your behavior in facing the situation.
Be the protagonist of your life. Choose good behavior and hold yourself accountable. Learn from the past and live in the present.

That's what 100% responsibility means. You are in control. No one to blame. No one will come to rescue you. You'll be fine.

Some questions that might help you:

- Who are you blaming for your life situation right now? (Your partner? Your boss? Your parents? Your friends?)
- What would happen if you stopped blaming others for what happens to you in your life?
- What benefits does it have for you to be a victim of your circumstances?
- What would happen if you took the decision to change your life NOW?
- What would you change? Where could you start? How would you start?

39

CHOICES AND DECISIONS

Everything in life happens for a reason, and sometimes the reason is that you make very bad decisions. I found this on social media, and it's meant as a joke, but there's actually a lot of truth in it. Your life is a result of the choices and the decisions you made. If you feel triggered by this statement, that's great because you have room for improvement.

Of course, bad things happen to good people but you still choose and, in the end, decide how these events will affect you. Yes. You really are this powerful!

Your life is a direct result of your past choices and decisions, and every choice carries a consequence. If you start making better choices, you will get better results. And if really bad things happen, then be like Viktor Frankl.

Victor Frankl was a Jewish psychologist imprisoned in Germany's concentration camps during the Second World War. He lost his entire family except for his sister. Under these horrible circumstances, he became aware of what he named "the ultimate human freedom," which not even the Nazi prison guards could take away from him: they could control his external circumstances, but in the last instance it was him **who CHOSE HOW these circumstances were going to affect him**! While he couldn't control the circumstances, he could choose his response in the face of these circumstances and so can YOU. This will make an enormous impact on your life.

So, whatever you're going through right now, know there is hope. You can overcome it. Maybe with the help of somebody (a therapist or coach). Nobody said you have to go through this alone.

What does this have to do with minimalism? I don't know. But better decision-making will make your life better.

Oh. Yes, now I remember. Minimalism and uncluttering are excellent for practicing your decision-making skills. If you follow Marie Kondo's method, you will start with small decisions like "Does this T-shirt spark joy?" "Do I really need 30 pairs of socks?" and you will make hundreds or even a thousand decisions—and what happens if you repeat something a thousand times? Right! You get better at it, and it gets easier.

At the end of the process, you get to the point where you have to decide on heavily emotionally packed items and have to ask again, "Does it stay or does it go?" This is a lot harder to decide, but you'll be great at making decisions then.

And then maybe the same happens to you as it did to me, and you'll start to decide who stays in your life and who has to go. Or whom you do business with. If you buy a certain course or not. It's truly magical. I got very good at decision-making, thanks to minimalism and uncluttering.

You would never believe it all started with the question, "Does this sock spark joy?"

40

SELF-DISCIPLINE AND COMMITMENT

Any new venture needs a bit of self-discipline and commitment. Without those two traits, it's doomed to fail or at best will take a lot longer. Your way to success is deeply connected to your willpower and commitment. These character traits will decide whether you do what you said you would do and go through with it. Self-discipline is doing the things you need to do, even if you are not in the mood for them.

They say self-discipline is like a muscle that can be trained and the more you train it, the better you get. As a matter of fact, for a long time I was convinced this was true. Well, I'm not 100% sure any more about self-discipline . . . Is it really self-discipline or is what looks like self-discipline only the right set of habits and routines.

Look at former athletes. They must be super self-disciplined, but some of them get super fat after they retire. So, did they lose their self-discipline or did they just stop doing healthy habits and routines?

So, if you don't have a lot of self-discipline, try habits. You need a lot less discipline for habits. Just in the beginning after a while the behavior becomes automatic and you'll just do it. The same way you brush your teeth.

Do you need self-discipline and motivation for brushing your teeth? No? Well, that's because it's a habit. Train to be self-disciplined or put in the right habits—or both.

What you do need is commitment. No commitment, no success —this is because commitment keeps you going. The secret to success is not so secret anymore. It's commitment and perseverance. Will you persevere in the face of adversity? That's the question.

And the best way to become successful in any endeavor is to start. So, stop thinking if you have self-discipline or not. Or if it's the habits. And simply go to work. And then again tomorrow. And the day after. Easy. Isn't it?

41

RAISE YOUR STANDARDS AND PROTECT YOUR BOUNDARIES

You teach people how to treat you by the way you treat yourself and by what you allow them. Keep your standards high and protect your boundaries.
Expect and demand more from yourself and from those around you. At first sight, this might have nothing to do with uncluttering and minimalism except that it does and a lot!

If you really want to make a positive change in your life, you have to raise your standards. Hold yourself to high standards and—what is of the same or even more importance—set boundaries for those around you. Decide to not accept mediocrity, procrastination, and behavior that impedes your best performance. Decide to always tell the truth, to always be punctual, to really listen to people until they are finished, and so on. The way you do the little things will define the way you do the big things so do the little things well.

Boundaries are things that people simply can't do to you. Show the people around you what you tolerate in relationships and what you don't. Communicate your boundaries clearly and make it a habit to address anything that bothers you on the spot. What are boundaries? Here are some examples: People can't yell at you, can't make stupid jokes around you or disrespect you, and—keeping what I mentioned before in mind—so can't you. Teach people by your example.

Defend your boundaries, and don't back down. If you back down, you're showing people you're accepting their behavior. For example, if you take a business call on Friday at 10 p.m., you're teaching the person that it's okay to call you for business at 10PM.

If somebody is overstepping your boundaries, call them out right away. **Inform** them: "I didn't like . . ." If they go on, **request** them to stop: "I ask you to stop . . . " By now most people should get it, but there are always one or two that continue. If that happens —**insist**: "I insist that you . . . " If all three steps don't help—**leave!** Walk away, neutrally stating, "I can't have this conversation while you are _____. Let's talk later."

The strength of your standards and boundaries will be reflected by your environment. Give it a try. Raise your standards and set boundaries.

Action Steps:

Write down the following things:

- Things you will no longer accept in your life.
- All the behaviors you will no longer tolerate from others.
- All the things you want to become.

42

SIMPLIFY

Simplify everything. Period. Simplifying brings freedom, joy, and balance. Once you enjoy your simple, uncluttered home, you'll never want to go back. On the contrary, you'll often catch yourself with questions like "What more can I simplify?" and "Where else can I remove distractions and simply focus on what's the most important?"

If you started applying some of the things that you have learned so far in this book, your life should already be a little simpler. Did you unclutter? Clean out your cupboard? Get rid of some tolerations? Did you get rid of some of the people that drag you down? Do you know your priorities? Did you make some time for the really important stuff in your life?

Minimalism is about downsizing your life and learning to live with less.

Life gets a lot simpler when you concentrate on the important stuff. The essential. The activities that make sense for you. Simply eliminate or downsize everything else. This can be done by automating, delegating, eliminating, or hiring help.

- Is your schedule too busy? Clear it out.
- Do you have too many commitments? Cancel or don't take on new ones.
- Can you simplify your financial life by using online banking?
- Start paying everything in cash and buy only things you really need?
- Spend less time on social media and more time in the real world with your friends and family.
- Check your emails only at certain times during the day and turn off the tone of email and text delivery so that you are not distracted all the time.
- Unsubscribe from journals that are just piling up and that you never read, and ask yourself if you really need to read three different newspapers every day.
- Are you commuting to work? Maybe you can ask your boss to work from home once or twice weekly.

Questions:

1. Where do you see the excess in your life?
2. Do you have too many things you don't need or use?
3. Is your schedule always booked?
4. Do you have time in your schedule for yourself and the things you enjoy doing?
5. What are the most important tasks in your day-to-day life (home and work)?
6. Which tasks can be easily delegated, automated, or eliminated?

43

START TO GET ORGANIZED!

As I mentioned before, minimalism isn't just getting organized. It's getting rid of unnecessary stuff. But organizing can be a first step, especially if you are insecure.

Marie Kondo tells you that you can just throw away all the papers you have in your house. That's even too bold for me. I mean, there can be important stuff. Taxes and the likes. So, I also chose to organize all the papers before throwing everything out. And here is the good news. Once I organized the papers, I noticed that I could throw at least 50% away without losing my sleep over it.

So if you are surrounded by mountains of paper and have Post-it notes all over your table in your office, it might be a good idea to look into this a bit.
There are studies that today's executives spend between 30% and 50% of their time searching for paperwork! Can you believe that?

So go and start organizing and filing papers and then throw the unnecessary ones away.
Clear your desk. It will increase your productivity
Journals and newspapers should go without even thinking about

it, and so should papers from courses that you did five years ago that you kept but never looked at again.

Did you know that digital clutter has the same effects as physical clutter? Your computer can be an awesome productivity tool but also the most distracting thing in your life. You choose.

One of my clients, Marc, did some virtual uncluttering, and it had the same effect on him as physical uncluttering. A big weight that he was carrying around was lifted from his shoulders and hence got a lot more energy.

The first thing he did was take control of his emails. Emails are such a huge time robber. As a matter of fact, you should get your most important work done every morning before looking at your emails, so don't check your emails first thing in the morning (except if your job relies on it, of course). This will make you a lot more productive.

Also, set fixed times for your social media activity and checking emails. Check your emails only at certain times during the day—for example at 9:00, 13:00, and 18:00 —and turn off all notifications, including email and text delivery, so you are not distracted.

After taking control of his emails, Marc uncluttered the desktop of his PC. He created folders on his desktop to sort documents. He deinstalled all unused software and apps.

In his email inbox, he first created a folder and put all the emails that were older than six months into it and then used it as a to-do list: answered emails were archived in their folders while unanswered emails stayed in the inbox. From then on, he cleared his email inbox every day.

He never looked back.

44

HARNESS THE POWER OF THE MORNING HOURS

This is not a book about time management, yet you found some little tricks for gaining more time in it. And I just can't help to put the habits that have helped me most into it. If you need more hours in your day to get everything done, you're not alone. I think most people think so.

One of the biggest game changers in my life—apart from gratitude, minimalism, and the 80/20 rule was introducing a morning routine. WOW. Incredible. Even though I do get lazy every now and then, if I really have to deliver or want to get a lot of work done, I go back to my morning routine. A morning routine will skyrocket your productivity and your well-being.

The most important hour of your day is composed of the thirty minutes after you wake up and the thirty minutes before you fall asleep. This is when your subconscious is very receptive, so what you do during this time is of great importance.

The way you start your day will have a huge impact on how the rest of your day develops. I'm sure you have had days that have started on the wrong foot and from then on got worse and worse —or the opposite where you woke up with that feeling that everything would go your way, and then it did. That's why it's very important to begin your day well. Most of us just get into a rush from minute one after waking up, and that's how our days unfold. No wonder most people run around stressed nowadays. What would getting up half an hour or an hour earlier every morning do for you?

When I was studying successful people, this was one of the main things they had in common. Some kind of morning routine. So, I thought, "If all these successful people have some kind of a morning routine there must be something to it. I better try." I tried and man did it change me.

While some people think that routines are boring and rigid, for me, it has been the way to productivity, freedom, and happiness.

My morning ritual when I need to deliver means getting up at 5 or 5:30 a.m. Walk for thirty minutes to clear my mind. Do my gratitude practice, a little meditation or just quiet time and look at what's most important for today (already figured out the day before, before going to sleep).

I have found that in the morning hours between 6 a.m. and 9 a.m. I can do double or triple the work I used to do because there are ZERO distractions and interruptions. Plus, there's a sense of accomplishment and pride when I see people going to work at 9 a.m., and I'm almost done for the day. This skyrockets my self-confidence because sticking to a plan/routine and achieving it feels good.

When you have a daily routine, you feel much more in control and probably feel less stress. You're creating a structure and good habits in your life. This will help you to get your priorities in order and gaining time in your day is all about priorities. Some other awesome "side effects" of having a morning routine are that it basically eliminates procrastination and creates momentum. Not to forget the important half an hour or hour of "me-time" you get by getting up earlier.

You can boost the results of your morning ritual if you add an evening ritual. The last half an hour of your day has the same importance. The things you do in the last half an hour before sleeping will remain in your subconscious during your sleep. Why not:

- Write into your journal
- Reflect on your day. (What did you do great? What could you have done even better?)
- Plan your day ahead. (What are the most important things you want to get done tomorrow?)
- Make a to-do list for the next day.
- Visualize your ideal day.
- Read some inspirational blogs, articles, or chapters of a book.
- Listen to music that inspires you.

I highly recommend that you NOT WATCH THE NEWS or MOVIES that agitate you before you are about to go to sleep. This is because when you are falling asleep, you are highly receptive to suggestions. That's why it's a lot more beneficial to listen or watch positive material.

Planning ahead for your day and getting together the list of things to do can bring you immense advantages and time savings. The things you have to do will already be in your subconscious, and you will get to work very focused the next day if you already know your priorities.
Will you give it a try? I highly recommend it!

45

USE THE MAGIC OF VISUALIZATION

Visualization is powerful. There's scientific proof that the subconscious part of your brain cannot distinguish between a well-done visualization and reality. Scientists scanned the brain of a subject when it was looking at its hand and then shortly after visualizing its hand. And what they saw on their brain scanner was mind-boggling. The areas of the brain that were "shooting" were the same in both cases.

So if you visualize your minimalism goals with a lot of emotion and in great detail, your subconscious mind will be convinced that it's really happening. It will then provide you with the motivation, opportunities, and ideas to help you transform your life into that desired state.

If you look at athletes and read their interviews, you'll find more proof that visualization really works if you do it regularly. Jack Nicklaus, Wayne Gretzky, and Greg Louganis—to name a few—are known to have achieved their goals with visualization.

In your visualization, you should envision yourself as already walking through your uncluttered house/apartment, having reached your minimalism goal. See it through your own eyes and put all your senses in it: smell it, hear it, feel it, taste it. The more emotions you put into it, the more of an impact it will have. If you do this for 15 minutes every day over time, you will see enormous results. Make time for your daily visualization either in your morning ritual or in the evening before going to bed.

It can be helpful to make a collage of images representing your goals on an A3 sheet of cardboard and put it up in your bedroom or somewhere you can see it. Buy some journals and cut out the photos that represent your goals. You could also create a screen-saver of various photos on your computer or desktop. If your goal is wealth, put a photo of your dream house, a photo of dollar bills, or whatever wealth means to you. If you search for "vision board" on Google, you will surely find many examples.
Look at your collage every day five minutes after getting up and five minutes before going to bed and imagine yourself vividly with your goal already accomplished.

Full disclosure. I'm not really good at visualization, and I'm living my dream life anyway. It's even better than I could ever imagine. Only three years ago, I lacked the imagination to visualize selling 100,000 books a year, living in a Penthouse on a beautiful island in the Mediterranean sea for one and a half years to then moving to live in one of Europe's most beautiful and vibrant capitals (Budapest, Hungary). I worked on my daily goals every day, did my gratitude exercise and other good habits, and things just "fell into place."

What I want to say is: Even if you're not good with visualization, you will still succeed if you have at least a slight idea of where you want to go, implemented some good habits in your life, have goals to achieve, and you put enough work into it. My personal philosophy always was that if you do the best you can every day, making small incremental progress, a year from now, you will automatically be in a great place. Imagine five years from now.

Action step:

What does your ideal environment look like? Use all your senses. What do you see? Hear? Smell? Touch? Taste? Jot down ideas and details and go to that place daily with your mind's eye.

46

THE POWER OF SMALL HABITS— CELEBRATE YOUR WINS!

This chapter is meant to cheer you up a little as we must never forget how far we've come already. There's always something to complain about (especially for the perfectionists among us); that's why we have to train our brains to see how great we've been doing so far. We have to learn to be aware of our progress.

So do me a favor and stop every now and then and celebrate how far you've come. Celebrate that you are better than you were last week and much better than last year. Congratulations to you!

Never ever let your small victories go unnoticed. Every action step completed; every little milestone reached is worth celebrating.

Reward yourself. Buy something you always wanted (after thinking about it and realizing that you really, really need it), go to the movies, or do whatever feels good for you and makes you happy.

I usually reward myself with short trips or a day in one of Budapest's marvelous spas. Smaller things, I celebrate with a cup of coffee in one of the various five-star hotels. Be creative! Will you have a spa day or a nice dinner? Will you go for a walk?

Write down some rewards here:

47

DO IT NOW!

The best way to achieve anything is to DO IT NOW. Don't wait for certain conditions or "a sign" to start doing. Start NOW with one little step in the right direction. I don't know a 100% surefire formula for success, but I surely know one for failure: Leaving things for later, aka procrastination.

If you have wanted to be a minimalist for the longest time and have never started to order your cupboard, you're probably procrastinating. Even reading more books on minimalism can be a form of procrastination. You must do yourself a huge favor and stop the procrastination.

It's such a pain. It causes anxiety and leaves you feeling bad most of the time. You will find out that the things you procrastinated on can actually be done in an hour. While some of my friends use procrastination to see things magically getting better after a while, this is rather the exception, and I wouldn't recommend it. Usually, things don't get better on their own, and many times they get worse.

Procrastinating is avoiding something that should be done. It's putting things off, hoping that they magically get better without actually doing anything about them. But even doing things that don't need to be done (instead of doing what you are supposed to be doing) or doing something that is more important than what you are supposed to be doing are forms of procrastination. Although the latter one probably won't do as much harm.

There is more as procrastination comes in a wide variety of forms: Getting distracted, putting off tasks, waiting until a task is perfect to complete it, or leaving everything up to the very last minute are other forms of procrastination.

Most of the time, the cause of procrastination is some kind of fear. Fear of rejection, fear of failure, fear of being judged, and even fear of success. Another cause is simply feeling over-whelmed.

It's amazing how many people are procrastinating by keeping themselves busy. They're making Excel sheets instead of sales calls. They design a master plan instead of just starting. I was always cleaning my room instead of studying for my exams.

You're paying a high price for procrastinating. Whenever you are tempted to put something off—in our case, probably decluttering —ask yourself: "What price will I be paying for procrastinating this task? Is it worth it to be burdened by and lose my sleep over a task that I could have finished in one or two hours?"

Don't take this lightly. Procrastination is dangerous. It usually ends in guilt, anxiety, self-loathing, or even depression, and it's damaging to the procrastinator's self-esteem and inner peace. This is a price far too high to pay.

As I mentioned before, the best antidote is to just START. Just

DO IT. The best way to overcome procrastination is to start. It's incredible how quickly you can get your brain from Procrastination Mode to productivity by just starting your task.

Whenever you use one of the following excuses, watch very closely! You might be procrastinating:

- "I'm too tired." (Just start. In five minutes, you won't be tired anymore)
- "I don't have time for it right now." (Yes, you do)
- "I need a break." (Take a 5 mins break and then start)
- "I don't feel like doing that now; I'll feel more like it later." (Just start)
- "It's too late to start this today; I'll do it tomorrow first thing." (Just start)
- "I have too many things on my plate." (Check your priorities)
- "I can't decide what to start with" (Just start)
- "It's not perfect" (It will never be. Start)
- "It's not the right time," "I'm waiting for the right moment" (The right moment is always NOW)

Here are some tips on what you can do to overcome procrastination:

Solutions:

- Be absolutely honest with yourself. If tempted to procrastinate, ask yourself, "What price am I paying for procrastinating this task?"
- Dive straight in (Action is the best antidote to procrastination).
- Focus on the results you'll get by doing the task you are tempted to leave for later.
- Focus on the rewards.
- Work with others (Coach, Accountability partner).

- Set yourself deadlines.
- Analyze, divide, and conquer tasks.
- Do the most uncomfortable task first thing in the morning.
- Focus on the task that brings in money.

Don't start tomorrow or next week! Start NOW!

48

PLANNING AND SCHEDULING

I'm sure you have heard great sayings like the following ones:

"If you spend half of your time planning, you will do everything twice as fast!"
"If you don't know where you are going, you can end up anywhere."
"If it's not in the calendar, it won't get done."

Maybe you have laughed about them or even made fun of them, "But that's sooo obvious," "Nothing new," "Common sense" . . . and then you have gone back to your stressed life, not having time hoping for a magical change in the future.

Well, as trivial as those phrases sound, they can change your life. Are you planning your days? Or are you just floating, fixing things as they turn up, putting out fires, and doing the same things every day? The habit of planning alone will probably already completely change your life.

Planning your days, weeks, and even months ahead will help you to put the right priorities in place and plan your important work.

The best way is to plan your week ahead on Sunday afternoon and "planning tomorrow today."

Make task lists. Put all of your upcoming tasks on there and assign a time to every single action on that list. Always have the list close by and visible. This will help you stay focused during the day. Another good idea is to work in blocks of time. I usually work in 90-minute blocks and then take a 30-minute break, or if I'm in the flow, three-hour blocks and then a two-hour break.

Ask yourself the three most important things you want to get done tomorrow, and don't forget to schedule free time, fun time, and travel time into your calendar and always leave a little reserve of time for emergencies that might come up.

Find time to start planning. Don't be too optimistic when you estimate how long a task will take. I usually double the time I think it takes. So if I think something takes an hour, I give it two hours in my schedule. This results in me always having more time than I need as I finish my tasks always in time. With this comes the psychological effect of having experienced the success of finishing tasks earlier, paired with rewards and well-being. You'll hardly ever see me stressed. For most people, the opposite happens. If you are too optimistic with your time, you'll "lose" time with every task taking longer than you thought, resulting in a heavy emotional weight that brings you down. A continuous feeling of failure to accomplish things which, in the end, attacks your self-esteem.

I plan my year, quarters, months, weeks, and days ahead, but I also give myself the freedom to change these plans, and you should do so, too. You're in charge. You can also choose not to follow the plan or make a new plan. The important thing is that planning gives you structure and direction.

The important thing is to book your activities into your calendar. Remember, "if it's not in the calendar, it won't get done."

Each evening, watch your calendar and see what your goals and actions for the next days are. This will make it so that the next day, you know exactly what to do and get to work directly instead of wasting precious time figuring out what to do.

Start planning. The rewards are awesome.

49

MINIMIZE DISTRACTIONS

Once the clutter is gone (clutter is a form of visual distraction) and you are well on your minimalist way, there will probably be the urge to get rid of more distractions.

Remember, the more things you own, the more time they are stealing from you because you're always organizing, cleaning, or changing places.

I know a lot of people who think and tell me that they are sooooo busy, work lots of overtime, and don't have any idea how and where to win time.

Once we look a little bit closer at their routine, we notice that they are checking their email every twenty minutes, getting notifications from people who saw their stuff on Facebook or Twitter, and are checking every new email that comes in every five minutes. Apart from this, they are surfing on the internet and watching YouTube videos and cat photos on Facebook.
The major difference between successful people and unsuccessful is their ability to not get distracted.
The Solution:

- Close your internet browser.
- Redirect your phone or take it off the hook.
- Turn off your mobile phone or at least turn the sound and notification sound off. (I usually put my phone on airplane mode to work productively and without interruptions or distractions.)
- Close your email. Don't check your emails regularly. (Three times a day for half an hour should be enough.)
- Log out of your social media networks.
- Set fixed times to be on Facebook, Twitter, etc. and stick to them.
- Close your office door.

Doing some of these things means an hour or two of time without being distracted by text messages or phone calls. Try it!

Once you start it, you'll love it. You'll notice that you'll get more things done than ever before. Just one or two hours a day can do miracles for your productivity.

If you are working from home, think very well who you let distract you. The person who wants to have coffee with you or take you to the mall will probably not be paying your bills at the end of the month when you wish back those hours that you lost being distracted and not doing what had to be done.

Another piece of advice . . . don't turn on the TV. You know it. Once it's on—gone is your productivity.

You can use the TV as motivation though: "If I get done what I planned for today, I'm going to reward myself with my favorite series."

50

THE 80/20 RULE

I love Vilfredo Pareto. His principle made my life so much better than you can even imagine it.

This might be one of the most important chapters for time management, minimalism, and productivity in the whole book.

Pareto's principle from the beginning of the 20th century was based on the discovery that 20% of the Italian population owned 80% of the land. And even though I doubted it for a while because today it's more like 1% own 99%, I can see Pareto's principle everywhere I look, and I have used it to minimize clutter and maximize productivity.

Pareto researched this ratio and also found it in his garden, where 20% of his tomato plants produced 80% of his tomatoes. So far so good.

Some smart people applied Pareto's principle to the business world and came up with the following:

80% of your results will come from 20% of your actions
80% of your profits come from 20% of your clients

80% of your complaints come from 20% of your clients
80% of your sales come from 20% of your products
80% of your sales come from 20% of your clients

Your business—and your available time—can grow exponentially
if you can concentrate on the projects that earn the most money
with the least time spent on them.

In my business that's definitely true.

80% of my income comes from 20% of my products.
80% of my sales come from 20% of my ads
20% of my ads spend 80% of my budget.
and so on . . .
It's amazing.

My success started when I concentrated on what brought 80% of
my income (Books) and then concentrated 80% of my time on
that (writing, producing, and promoting books)

Applied to minimalism:

I noticed I spent 80% of the time in 20% of my house (that helped
me with my decision to move onto a boat).

I noticed I only wore 20% of my T-shirts (I had 50 T-shirts at a
time, now I have 18 and guess what . . . I'm always wearing the
same six or seven . . .).
Same with trousers and so on

I'm pretty sure it's the same for you. Correct me if I'm wrong, of
course. This would mean that 80% of your clothes can go if you
are hardcore like me, or at least 40% if you want to take it slower.

You might find the 80:20 rule all over your cupboard, your bathroom, your kitchen, and even your paperwork. If I could, I'd bet on it.

So, sit down and identify everything in your house and your workplace or business using Pareto's Principle. Apply the 80/20 rule to every area of your business and your personal life. You can thank me later.

51

TURN OFF YOUR PHONE

Talking about having less things. How about having fewer phone calls or better said, less time robbed by your phone. Do you answer every phone call? Well . . . don't! Let it go to voicemail every now and then. Turn off your phone and put it in another room. You can't? You're going to lose the client? Yeah. I heard that one a lot. Basically, from every person I told to do this. Never happened though. Leave a nice message on your voice mail in the sense of the good old, "Sorry I'm busy and can't get your call right now. I'll call you back as soon as possible."

Of course, your situation might be different so you decide. I don't want you to be fired from your job because you stop answering the phone. But you know what I mean. Let the phone go to voicemail more often when you can. If it's an important call they will call again. Or they will leave a message. Or you'll see their number on your display and call them. The only thing that's really bad is not calling them back right after you have finished what you are doing or even forgetting them.

Not picking up the phone every time it rings brings you an enor-mous amount of time and all the benefits that come with it like better productivity, more time to reflect, more happiness. Give it a try.

One of my clients, a very stressed sales manager, let's call him Steve, came to me at the edge of being seriously burnt out. He received 60 to 80 calls a day and didn't have time to do his real job which was selling his product and visiting customers, because he was on the phone all the time fixing everyone's problems and continuously putting out fires. He also thought he'll lose clients and consequently his job but he was at the brink of a breakdown anyway so he gave it a shot. He decided to let calls go to voice mail for at least an hour every day and changed the message of his voice mail. "Hi. I can't get to the phone right now. I'll call you back as soon as I can. If it's urgent send me a WhatsApp message." That's it.

The first two weeks nothing happened. In the third week he suddenly received only half the calls and by the time he called back 80% of the problems people called for in the first place were fixed. He also had zero urgent WhatsApp messages. After a month he was relaxed. He thought he might have received fewer calls because vacation time was close by or work was slow. Three months later he had to admit to himself that he did it! He was in control of his time. He also improved his free time with his family on the weekends because he wasn't thinking about work all the time and had time to think about fun stuff to do with his family.

Further he went on to break his company's sales records for a couple of years and then he joined the sales team of a competitor who treated him a lot better than his old boss. **All this nine months after deciding to not answer the phone every time it rings. Magical.**

52

TURN OFF YOUR TV

Minimize everything. One huge game changer will be turning off your TV.

Studies say that the average American spends 4 to 5 hours a day in front of the TV, and the same goes for Europeans. The younger generations probably watch less TV but are glued to the screen anyway watching Netflix, Disney+, HBO Max, YouTube or social media.

That means the average person is watching between 28 and 35 hours of TV (or any of the above mentioned) a week.

TV is one of the biggest energy drainers, if not the number one. It keeps you in a trance. Do you ever feel renewed or reenergized after watching TV (except if you watched an awesome motivational speech of course)?

TV is a source of negativity and garbage and won't help you, except if you use it to watch content that can actually help you. I blame TV for the mass panic we lived through in the last two years.

Don't misunderstand me. There was a Pandemic. But if the media would count every death from car accidents or flu, we'd be afraid to go out of the house by now. Did you notice that with all the other illnesses the counter goes back to zero every year? Cancer deaths, drug deaths, flu deaths. At the end of the year, the counter goes back to zero. Just COVID keeps accumulating. I wonder why that is . . .

Anyways. Turn off your TV and enjoy the new won time that you can use for taking walks, reading good books, more time with family and friends, more time in the real life (TV is strongly biased to show us the negative stories), more time at the gym, more FUN, and a lot more.

If you are really addicted to your box, start slowly and watch less TV (although I recommend you go cold turkey). Just try it for yourself! Don't watch TV for a week and see how you feel.

No worries. You will still be up to date with the important stuff because your family, friends, and colleagues will keep you updated. Just choose and be selective about how much garbage you expose your mind to. There are even studies that say that people who don't watch TV are actually better judges of reality than people who watch it.

If you need more reasons to stop watching television, read one of the great books that are out there about how the media manipulates us and how nearly everything is fake! Control the information that you are exposed to. Make sure it adds to your life. Instead of watching trash TV, watch a documentary or a comedy. Instead of listening to the news in your car, listen to an audiobook or motivational CD.

Here are some experiences I have had with the media:

- Radio programs recorded on a Wednesday and sold as

"live" on a Sunday. I couldn't speak about it, not post about it on social media etc. until Sunday

- Great speeches from the anchor written by someone else and read from a teleprompter.
- When I was a guest on a talk show, I got the questions one day in advance so I could prepare myself very well.
- A famous radio host read the whole show from a script that other people wrote for him.

Stop watching TV and enjoy the benefits of the minimalist lifestyle.

53

WHAT'S THE MOST IMPORTANT THING?

Establish priorities. What's the most important thing? Do this first every morning. I bet you can make amazing and unimaginable progress if you do the three most important things every day.

Yup. That's enough. If you do the three most important things in your life every day in one year, you'll be in a completely different —a much better—place. The difficult thing is to find out what are these three things every day.

Make your list of priorities now and every evening before going to bed. Why before going to bed? Because then your subconscious mind will work on it during your sleep, and when you wake up the next day, you'll be focused, know exactly what to do, and get right to work. Sounds crazy? Try it. You'll be surprised.

Knowing your priorities is the only way to make time. It's always about priorities. When I talk to other coaches, we never say, "Oh, I don't have time." This is because we know the other person understands, "You are not as important to me as this other thing." And it's okay. That's life.

You will never have enough time to fit in everything you have to do in one day. The day you will have time when you leave things for "when I have time" will also never come. It's all about priorities and choices. The sooner you get it, the better. The fun thing is when you start prioritizing and making choices sooner or later, you will have enough time.

So, what's the most important thing for you right now?

54

ME TIME

When you have less stuff, you have more time. Fewer clothes are more quickly laundered and ironed (I don't even iron, so I save even more time). Less stuff is more quickly put away. So, what happens then? You'll have more time. I highly recommend you to use at least some of that time as "Me-time." Time that is yours and for you. You can use it to read a good book, meditate, write down five things you're grateful for, or just do what you want to do. This is extremely important. It will calm you down and make you happier in the long run. Self-care is very important, and "Me-time" is a big chunk of that.

As the unnecessary stuff leaves your house or apartment, you have more time to listen to yourself. You'll be able to focus and think. You'll stop running around like a headless chicken from one urgency to the next one.

I can't promise that there will be no more long, exhausting, stressed days once you adopt minimalism as a lifestyle, but there'll surely be a lot less.

Use that newly gained time and transform a lot of it into "Me time." There's something magical to valuing your time. The more you value your time, the more other people will value your time, and you'll have . . . more time.

55

GET RID OF INTERRUPTIONS

How many times do you get interrupted each day? If you allow people to interrupt you, you'll be unable to work effectively, no matter how many hours you work. Studies have found out that each 5-minute interruption at work costs you 12 to 32 minutes because your brain needs 7 to 25 minutes to refocus! How many interruptions do you have per day? 10? 12? How much time can you save if you decrease the number of interruptions? How? Set clear rules when people can interrupt you. For example, make clear rules when people can call you or take the phone off the hook (airplane mode for the younger readers) for three hours and get more work done because you're laser-focused. Turn off the emails, notifications, and don't even try to multitask because multitasking is a lie and makes you dumber!

A study by the University of London found that if you keep your email open while doing concentrated work, it's like taking off 10 IQ points from your IQ. TEN POINTS!!!

That's the same effect as going 36 hours without sleep. Did you ever work after going 36 hours without sleep? And how did that go? I guess not very well . . . On a side note: Smoking marijuana only reduces the IQ by 4 points.

This can be difficult to apply when you work in a corporate office, but it can be done. Nothing will happen if you turn your email off for two to three hours; nothing will happen if your phone is off for two to three hours (unless you are an ambulance driver or a doctor).

In case of interruptions by your colleagues or even your boss, make it clear when you are available and when not. Do the same with emails and phone calls and find a way that people can get to you in an emergency (WhatsApp, special email address, etc.)

If people at work or your boss won't believe you about the importance of working without distraction, gift them a copy of one of my other books *The Productivity Revolution* or *Destination Happiness"* or tell them to invite me to your company to speak.

You can also take a photo of this chapter and send it to them. People usually don't like time management tricks even if they don't have time. Because this is the ugly truth and the truth sometimes hurts. If you are ready to take the pain and follow the tips, your life will get better.

I promise.

56

SAY "NO" AND SAY IT OFTEN

Minimalists say "NO" a lot and to many things. When you start uncluttering, you say "NO" to many things that can't stay in your cupboard, your bedroom, your living room and so on. Further along the way, you will say no to highly emotionally charged items and even people and business relationships. And that's okay because your life will improve along the way.

When you learn to say "NO" and stop trying to please everyone else, you're actually saying yes to your new YOU and your new lifestyle.

When a "No" is a "No"—and not a yes just to please others, freedom and authenticity begins. The "Yes" becomes stronger, more honest, more mindful, and more committed and thus more valuable.

Learn to say "NO" without feeling guilty. The uncluttering process will help a lot because you will say "No" many times. Once you start saying "No" to people, you can explain to the person in question (it's not anything personal against them) or not. It's up to you. You don't owe anyone an explanation or justification.

I know that sounds a bit selfish, doesn't it? And it is! But keep in mind who the most important person in your life is. That's right! YOU are the most important person in your life. You have to be well. Only if you are well yourself can you be well towards others, and from this level, you can contribute to others, but first be well yourself.

Successful people say "NO" a lot, productive people say "NO" a lot, happy people say "NO" a lot. Minimalists say "NO" a lot. See a pattern?

Life gets a lot better if you start saying "NO"! And once you regularly do so, you are well on your way to becoming a Minimalist.

CONCLUSION

Here we are! Already at the end of the book. That was quick, wasn't it? Did you start uncluttering already, or did you first read the book superficially and will now go through it again and take action?

I'm glad I started uncluttering back in 2016/2017, and look how far I've come. The great thing is: If I can do it, you can do it. Maybe in a different way—YOUR WAY—but I'm sure you'll be able to enjoy the benefits that come with it.

I was pretty bold with the title and subtitle of this book: *The Happy Minimalist*. How to create a simpler, more organized, more joyful life and achieve inner peace. That's a lot of promises. I hope I met your expectations or, at best, even exceeded them. As you follow the steps to minimalism, you should become less stressed and happier along the way. These are the "side effects" I have experienced and all the minimalists that I have met or read.

Of course, you have to do the work. And careful: becoming happier and experiencing less stress doesn't mean that unhappiness, sadness, and stress will totally disappear from your life.

They are part of life and will show up every now and then, but you'll be able to deal with them better.

Ah. I owe you some book recommendations. These are the books that helped me most on my way:

- *The Magic of Tidying up*—Marie Kondo
- *Simplify*—Joshua Becker
- *Clear your Clutter with Feng Shui*—Karen Kingston
- *10-Minute Declutter*—S.J. Scott, Barrie Davenport
- *Minimalism*—The Minimalists
- *Essentialism*—Greg McKeown.

What? Only six books? Yes. Actually, ONE is enough. Remember: The most important thing is to START DOING—not only reading many books on minimalism. So, I hope you have already started your journey toward minimalism.

So, what will minimalism look like to you? Let me know. I answer all my emails (except the ones that troll or ask me for money). You can write me at marc@marcreklau.com. I usually get back within 48 hours (not on weekends, though).

All the best!
Marc

P.S. If you liked the book, it would be awesome if you could leave a review on Amazon or wherever you bought it. It helps other readers to find the book—and me to get better promotion opportunities and sell more books. :)

ABOUT THE AUTHOR

Marc Reklau is a Coach, Speaker, and author of 12 books including the international Bestsellers "30 Days - Change your habits, change your life", "Love yourself First" and "How to become People Magnet". His books have sold over half a million copies and have been translated into 15+ languages including Spanish, German, Japanese, Chinese, Russian, Thai, Indonesian, Portuguese and Korean.

He wrote his first book 30 DAYS in 2014 after being fired from his job and literally went from jobless to Amazon Bestseller (which is actually the title of his second book).

Marc's mission is to empower people to create the life they want and to give them the resources and tools to make it happen.

His message is simple: Many people want to change things in their lives, but few are willing to do a simple set of exercises constantly over a period of time. You can plan and create success and happiness in your life by installing habits that support you on the way to your goals.

You can connect with him via email (marc@marcreklau.com) on Instagram @MarcReklau or on Linkedin.

Marc reads all his emails and answers most of them - except the rude ones.

ALSO BY MARC REKLAU